Sustainable Business

High-Impact Business Innovation Series

Edited by
CJ Meadows

Volume 2

CJ Meadows

Sustainable Business

—

People, Profit, and Planet at The Tiger Center

DE GRUYTER

SPJ GLOBAL — S P Jain School of Global Management

DUBAI · MUMBAI · SINGAPORE · SYDNEY

The Tiger Center

TIGERCENTER.ORG

ISBN 978-3-11-078294-3
e-ISBN (PDF) 978-3-11-078317-9
e-ISBN (EPUB) 978-3-11-078327-8
ISSN 2700-7847

Library of Congress Control Number: 2023939453

Bibliographic information published by the Deutsche Nationalbibliothek
The Deutsche Nationalbibliothek lists this publication in the Deutsche Nationalbibliografie;
detailed bibliographic data are available on the internet at http://dnb.dnb.de.

© 2023 Walter de Gruyter GmbH, Berlin/Boston
Typesetting: Integra Software Services Pvt. Ltd.
Printing and binding: CPI books GmbH, Leck

www.degruyter.com

Advance Praise for *Sustainable Business*

Inspiring and timely! If you care about sustainability, innovation, impact investing, social enterprise, not-for-profit organizations/NGOs, or just generally making our world better – this is the book for you.

–**Virginia Cha**,
Global Agenda Council Member,
World Economic Forum

A must-read for every corporate executive interested in ESG, CSR, and emerging market expansion. The content is invaluable for government and conservation leaders, too!

–**Dr. Asli Chamizo-Toksal**,
Sustainability, AI, and
Innovation Consultant and Board Director

A watershed work! Environmentalists and economists have much to learn from each other, and this book both uncovers the synergies and provides a practical scorecard for management. Fascinating expose of how vastly different people work together for common good.

–**Prof. Nishikant Mukerji**,
Member, Wildlife Ecotourism Board of Maharashtra;
Director, Center for Science in Villages

A passionate personal story of tigers, environment, and people! This book also provides larger lessons for all social entrepreneurs who seek a better balance between people, economics, and the natural environment.

–**Dr. Chris Marshall**,
VP – Data Analytics, AI, Resiliency, and
Sustainability, IDC Asia Pacific

An inspiring story of people, passion, and purpose coming together for the betterment of our planet! With deep insights on innovation and entrepreneurship, Dr. Meadows takes us on a journey to magnificent tigers, indigenous tribes, and success fueled by community partnership.

–**Priya Rath**,
Sustainability, Agriculture,
Product Management, and Partnerships Leader, Bayer

https://doi.org/10.1515/9783110783179-202

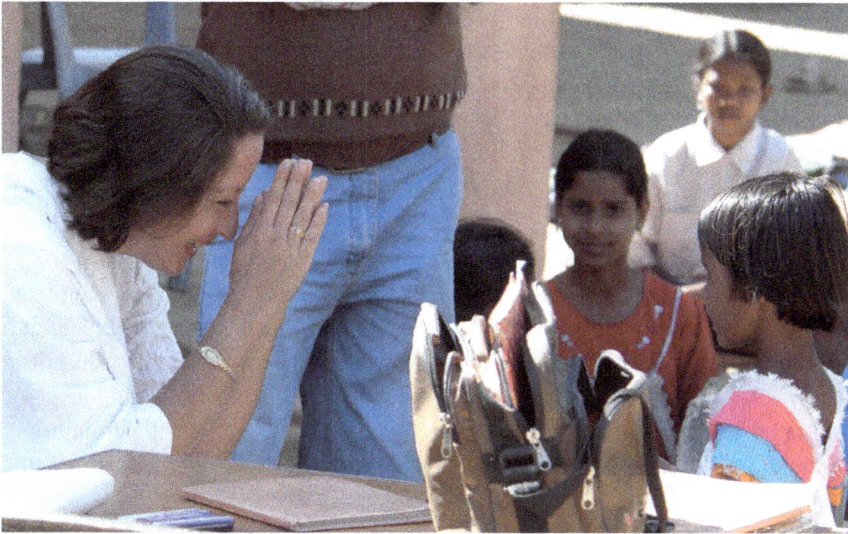

Figure 0.1: The author at a school event in Kanha.

Acknowledgements

My first thanks, as always, goes to God. This time, He not only gave me ideas, inspiration, and the ability to communicate with you, but He gave us the subject matter of this book, as well – the Earth and a social enterprise that works to sustain its creatures, the environment, and His children (see Figure 0.1).

Speaking of children, I thank my children – Jonathan, Anna, David, and Sarah – for being a key reason to write about the world I'll be leaving in their hands. I pray they steward it better than the generations that have gone before them (including mine) and ask their forgiveness for leaving them with an ecological problem. That said, it's one which we are currently able to solve, if we foster the political, economic, and grassroots will and learn to work together. Scientists tell us that window of opportunity won't last long – certainly not beyond my children's lifetime.

I thank my husband, Chris Marshall, and helper, Gisela Cabalang, for your never-ending support. Only with your help can I spend time not only writing but also addressing these challenges that impact us all and our most valued resource – our families.

I thank Nitish Jain and the S P Jain School of Global Management for the encouragement and time to write books such as these. You and the institution you founded care about impact and developing new ways to make the world better

https://doi.org/10.1515/9783110783179-203

through new knowledge and education. We need new knowledge assets and in-spired, informed leaders to transform ideas into reality.

Thank you, Nandu Bhau (Anand Jagdale), for your friendship, your leader-ship, your role in the very first Tiger Center story (how the land was acquired), and your hard work, support, and facilitation through the years. We're proud to have known you and worked alongside you. We pray for you and your family. We miss you and always will.

In fact, when Bhau passed away, there was some concern about how we could carry on, especially since so much of the organizing had been done from Nagpur. When the team in Kanha called to inquire about Bhau's wellbeing and were informed that he'd passed away, without hesitation they told Nishi not to worry. They would ensure that everything that needed to be done would be done, and organizing and operations would continue from Kanha itself. Without any prompting to do so, they immediately closed the schools and operations for a day of mourning.

Special thanks go to that early team for their collective leadership, including Sudhir Puranik, Ramesh Mehta, Ashish Kachwaha, Rano and Babita Lakhera, Salim Quershi, Mallu Singh, Kura Bai Chhapri, Sonsay Baiga, and Sukhman.

I thank the whole team at The Tiger Center (TTC) – past and present – with-out whom this book would only be a treatise on what others understand. We un-derstand more by not only reading and listening, but by working with our hands, connecting with people, and being the change we wish to see in the world (yes, Gan-dhi said that first and encouraged us to do so). Without you, there would be no new model of conservation, no on-the-ground eco-tech promotion in our community, and no lives saved or wellbeing improved with our people programs. You're the hands that make it work. I just sing your praises and help in the little ways I can.

I include in my thanks those who are part of TTC "in memoriam." I wish you could have seen the growth you inspired and worked for.

A special thanks goes to Sami Mohammad for being a good steward of the land that would become ours and for offering it to Nishi in just the right way, at just the right time.

Thank you, Chris Marshall, for the inspirational conversation with Nishi that gave birth to the early Tiger Center mission and vision, as well as your financial support of TTC over the years.

Thank you also, Nishi, for leading TTC as an operating organization all these years and for (1) discussing with me what would be the contents of this book; (2) key conversations and ideas while writing (like your Golden Triangle Balanced Scorecard idea); and (3) reviewing and improving it before publication.

I thank the Forestry Service and the Baiga, Gond, and village communities we work with. Not only are you the first line of defense to protect tigers and environment, but you taught us that people have to be part of the conservation equation. You shared with us your priorities – healthcare, education, and economic sustenance. You've inspired our mission, guided and facilitated our efforts, and helped us focus our future efforts on scalable, global initiatives that begin with you.

Thank you, research assistants Eswar Krishnan and Sai Vithal Valluri. Your work has made this book more informative, more up-to-date, and more relevant than I could have made it. Someone in the future will be lucky to have you advise them, and I'm grateful for the illumination you've given me.

Thank you, Stefan Giesen, Jaya Dalal, and the whole team at De Gruyter. You're a terrific team to work with, and I thank you for your patience and never-ending help.

Do forgive me, please, if I've missed someone. It takes a village to write a book, even though one name goes on the front.

Finally, thank you, dear readers. I pray this book will assure you that we can make a difference to both Earth and ourselves in ways that benefit endangered species, environment, and people – and, ultimately, the whole planet. I pray that the social enterprise insights will help you with whatever initiatives you launch.

We depend on each other more than we know and can help each other more than we realize.

Contents

About the Author

Awarded as one of Asia's Top 10 Women in IT, Dr. Meadows leads an Innovation and Entrepreneurship Center at Forbes Top 20 International Business School S P Jain School of Global Management, creating growth initiatives at the intersection of IT, business strategy, and design. Her research, consulting, teaching, and coaching focus on design thinking, leadership, creativity, and the Future of Work (FoW) and Education.

She co-founded and chairs The Tiger Center (TTC), a not-for-profit corporation focusing on economic growth with environmental sustainability and social welfare. Its mission is to Help the Tiger, Help the Environment, and Help the People. TTC's new model of conservation, integration of economy and ecology, community programs, future direction as an EdTech and MedTech incubator, and more are outlined in these pages.

Holding a doctorate in business administration and IT from Harvard Business School, she has over 25 years' experience in Asia, Europe, and North America as a consultant, coach, entrepreneur, eBusiness builder, innovation lab co-founder, and Accenture IT and Business Strategy consultant.

https://doi.org/10.1515/9783110783179-205

Introduction and How Sustainable Business Can Help You

Figure 0.2: The world reflected in the eyes of a baby langur monkey.

> One does not meet oneself until one catches the reflection from an eye other than human.
> — Loren Eiseley

If you're looking for a generic tome on sustainability, keep looking. This book includes information on sustainability and business you probably won't find elsewhere, but it is mainly a story of innovation and of one highly innovative sustainable business venture.

You'll want to continue reading this book if you're interested in sustainability, green economics, social enterprise, rural business, or innovation (see Figure 0.2). Keep reading if you're interested in not-for-profit organizations (NPOs) or non-governmental organizations (NGOs).

It's interesting to consider that we describe them by saying what they're "not." Perhaps we don't understand well enough what they are.

Keep reading, as well, if you're interested in tigers, a majestic animal and great spokesman. If you find all of the above interesting, then all the better.

In this book, we'll explore:

https://doi.org/10.1515/9783110783179-206

- facts, figures, and synergies between people, profit, and planet particular to this venture but generalizable, as well, to other species, other locations, and other organizations
- the journey of one organization working at the intersection of all three
- broader understanding of the different facets and levels of "sustainability": planet, profit, people, and person. Sustainability of individual health and energy is a key issue for everyone, especially women who care for businesses and families, whether as a corporate chairman or a farmer

With this work, I hope to reveal insights you can apply to your own growing enterprises and ecological circumstance, fostering more powerful economic and ecological synergies and success.

The High-Impact Business Innovation Series (of which this is Book 2) began with *Famous Business Fusions*. All the books in the series explore different facets of "fusion."

What's fusion (lateral innovation)?

Basically, in nuclear fusion, two nuclei come together to form a new one, thereby releasing a great deal of energy into the world. Likewise, in business, science/technology, and the humanities, when you bring together currently-disparate fields, industries, nations, technologies, social classes, or other fodder for innovation, it's fertile ground for creating radical innovation that releases a great deal of value into the world.

Why is this book a fusion story? First, most people think sustainability initiatives will be more costly to business and thereby damaging. Often, the reverse is true, encouraging leaders to discover and eliminate waste, take advantage of hitherto unseen synergies, and seeing (maybe for the first time) ecological resources as assets to protect and make productive.

Economy and environment can integrate and release a great deal of value into the world.

Second, we examine the work and growth of a social enterprise – The Tiger Center (TTC) – working at the intersection of endangered species, environment, and people. Both the topic that this book addresses and TTC include the following fusions:

- People, profit, and planet
- "Eco-development" that includes economy AND ecology
- Theory (a new conservation model) and practice (grassroots action and case examples)
- Business, not-for-profit, government, academe, and community working together

- Family and business – a reflection of the co-founders' "Fusion Family" (see The Fusion Family TEDx video, Meadows [2015])
- Multi-faith inclusiveness
- National origin
- Fields
- People from different "walks of life" working together, from Baiga tribals to global executives
- People from the four ages of man working together (Baiga hunter-gatherer, Gond agricultural, village and team industrial age, and team information age)
- Men and women
- Multi-generational collaboration (team members range from teenage through 76)
- Team members who themselves are "fusioney" (multi-national, multi-field, multi-industry, etc.)
- "High-tech" and "low-tech" working together (e.g., social media promotion and WhatsApp coordination of traditional tribal activities, medical camps, etc.)
- Size – a small organization working with large businesses and government

In addition to serving as Chairman of TTC, I also oversee other family businesses, coach my four kids (no longer homeschooling now that they're in university), and am a full-time professor, leading an innovation and entrepreneurship center. What more appropriate book topic could this author choose than a book on an innovative, entrepreneurial business I co-founded, in which my kids take part? Professors are tasked with creating and sharing new knowledge, so I'd like to share with you the new ideas, insights, and lessons we've learned.

It was actually hard to organize this book, since people, profit, and planet operate in synergy (or should, anyway). So how to write a linear narrative? I'll start with planet (the big picture), then move to profit (a more focused endeavor) and people (who both benefit from planet and profit, as well as fostering or damaging them). Each chapter will include some of the other elements, since they're intertwined.

Actually, I guess that's the point.

Wherever figures were reported in currencies other than USD, I've translated them for the reader to USD using a 2023 first-quarter spot rate.

Digital resources can be found at drcjmeadows.com/sustainability, and you can see videos and learn more about The Tiger Center at tigercenter.org. A companion multimedia book will also be available at GnowbeLearn™ (learn.gnowbe.com) and listed on the above web pages. In the multimedia book, you can watch videos, answer reflective questions designed to help you apply insights to your own situation, and connect with a community of readers/viewers immersed in the same material, applying it to their own lives, too. One thing I've learned on this sustainability journey is that community makes the journey more sustainable.

Nature operates in an ecosystem, and so do people and their organizations.

Photos are by either Prof. Nishikant Mukerji or me, unless otherwise noted. They were taken in the course of our work at The Tiger Center over the last two decades. A few images, like the pawprint and the Vespa rider in the blue turban, are copyright-free purchased images from depositphotos.com. Naresh Yadav (thank you!) kindly donated the use of the tigress and her 5 cubs at the beginning of the Conclusions chapter. Krishna Photos (thank you!) kindly donated the use of the final image – the tiger who appears to be waving "bye-bye."

Thank you for your interest, your time, and all the good you'll do to make our world more sustainable. I pray this material will help you do so.

Chapter 1
The Man with the Blue Turban

> Let your hook always be cast; in the pool where you least
> expect it, there will be a fish.
> — Ovid

Walking together along a forest road, listening to and breathing in the sounds and scents of nature, Nishi and Bhau saw a tiny blue speck far along the road.

They stood and watched.

Soon, they could see it wasn't a blue speck. It was a blue-turbaned man on a motorbike.

"I hear you're looking for land. Would you like to buy my family's land? It's just on the edge of the nature reserve – the only privately held land around here."

Nishi said he'd be interested but would have to get back to him. The man (Sami Mohammad), Bhau, and Nishi exchanged contact details. Investigation showed that sure enough, the land was the only privately held (non-tribal) land near the reserve.

This was something special.

Nishi recalled how he got to this point in his life.

He'd been hand-picked to advise and assist the leadership of one of India's most prestigious companies. He cautioned against what could be construed as lapses in governance and strategic controls that could cause serious problems downstream.

When he saw that there was no change in the status quo and that ominous storm clouds were gathering – signs of a crisis – he relocated to his *alma mater*, the Asian Institute of Management (AIM) in the Philippines, as a full-time professor of strategic management. He taught, built a new life, and later became the program director of their flagship 2-year MBA program.

I met him there while getting my doctorate at AIM's founding organization, Harvard Business School. He began going to church again with me, and we grew closer. Soon, we were brother and sister. (In India, a girl who has no brother can choose one. It's formalized in a ceremony called Raksha Bandhan.)

It took ages, but his former employer finally paid his final salary.

It was time to move on, build a new life, and think about what was really important – to himself and others.

So, he went back with his childhood friend Anand Jagdale (Nandu Bhau) to a place he had loved during his childhood – Kanha Nature Reserve, one of Indira Gandhi's original nine Project Tiger nature reserves. They were scouting for land (for a

https://doi.org/10.1515/9783110783179-001

vacation or retirement home for Nishi) but made it clear they would not buy tribal land. Only a tribe member can legally build on tribal land, unless the whole tribe agrees – and there's always someone who arrives later saying they weren't asked.

Nishi decided to buy, asked the price, and was stunned.

It was the same amount (almost to the rupee) that his former company had paid him – his final salary and benefits.

He wanted the land not only because it was superb, but because he felt God was nudging him to buy the land and do something important with it.

He didn't know what.

Nishi and Bhau eventually partnered with friends and family to build an organization that would help tigers thrive and multiply, impact public environmental policy, save and improve lives, and more. Sami Mohammad – an influential local leader (sarpanch) – became an important supporter.

Many years later, both Bhau and Sami passed away, but Nishi continued to work for tigers, the environment, and people – and does so to this day.

He took a leap of faith and has been walking that road ever since.

Chapter 2
Planet

Environment

Before Adam Smith published his seminal book *The Wealth of Nations* in 1776, he published *The Theory of Moral Sentiments* in 1759. It's easy to mistake his fervor for individual freedom, competition, free-market economics, and capitalism as a system in a vacuum.

However, his economic work was written after – and assumed a foundation of – his moral work. The ethics he presents in *The Theory of Moral Sentiments* can be applied not only to human relations but also to our relations with our environment. *The Wealth of Nations* and our economies do not operate in a vacuum. Nor do we.

Indeed, the wave of attention businesspeople have paid recently to ethical concerns, including environment, social, and governance (ESG) issues ironically generated economic activity. It spawned a new industry – ESG consulting. After infatuation and growth, ESG entered a period of controversy over whether ESG efforts and investments (including consulting fees) are actually worthwhile. We examine it with green accounting and triple-bottom-line metrics, and then choose a side to argue.

I'll not rehash the arguments here or give a treatise on green economics. Others have done a much better job than I currently can. All I'll say on the topic is this: we cannot run our economies in a vacuum forever, because there's another vacuum in which they operate – Earth.

Our planet recycles our mistakes and brings them back to us.

https://doi.org/10.1515/9783110783179-002

Scientists have clearly linked the state and rate of climate change to human/ economic activity. That said, we have clearly shown that we can gather the political will to reverse some of the damage we've done. The big win example is the ozone hole above Antarctica. After banning chlorofluorocarbons (CFCs), the hole is repairing and expected to heal by 2066 (Newburger, 2023).

But do we have the business will to manage our economy and ecology together, for further wins?

Natural capitalism and the idea that it could be the next industrial revolution (Hawken et al., 2000) made a huge impression on what would later become our first leadership team – Bhau, Nishi, my husband (Chris Marshall), and me. Nishi investigated further (with a little help from the rest of us) and wrote two whitepapers (both 2009) – one called "EDEN: Economic Development with Environmental Nurturing" and the other titled "Managing Natural Assets."

What we learned with those first two whitepapers surprised us. Apparently, at the time, the biggest industry in the world (for income generation and employment) after oil was travel and tourism, and the fastest-growing segment was eco-tourism – wildlife and adventure.

Fast forward 9 years to 2018, and global tourism continued to grow, outperforming global economic growth for the eighth consecutive year –

including construction, healthcare, retail, and wholesale (Yes Bank Strategic Government Advisory and FICCI, 2019). It accounted for 10.4% of global GDP and contributed USD 8.81 trillion to the global economy (USD 2.75 trillion directly).

Travel provided 10% of global employment (319 million jobs), and 20% of all new jobs created during the previous 5 years were in tourism.

India was the 8th largest contributor to global travel and tourism GDP, providing 27 million jobs (43 million, including indirect jobs) and USD 247 billion at 6.7% growth – 9.2% of its economy overall. Global travel and tourism was the third-largest foreign exchange earner for the country, at USD 29 billion.

Today, different reports place travel and tourism in various spots in the global top 10 industries. According to the World Travel and Tourism Council (2022, using 2021 figures), tourism generated USD 170 billion in India alone (5.8% of its GDP), supporting 32 million jobs. Growth is predicted at a healthy 7.8% per annum.

Whether the travel and tourism segment is #1 or merely in the top 10, it is economically important. We need to pay attention, manage it well, and leverage it for growth and wellbeing.

When people do travel to or within India, what do they want to see? Many would say the Taj Mahal and the tiger. The tiger is enough of an attraction that former Prime Minister Dr. Manmohan Singh, an eminent economist, said India's tiger reserves should be managed as profit centers.

Does that mean a reserve that doesn't turn a profit will be shut down? We doubt that, since they also support missions of conservation and research, as well as supplying life-sustaining eco-services (described more fully below).

Profitability doubts notwithstanding, what if we did manage the reserves as profit centers? Any business manager or leader can tell you that measures and targets can drive (or at least direct) performance. Without measures of how efficiently the assets are managed and what returns are gathered from them, it would be hard (or impossible) for the reserves to reach their full potential. (FYI, the Taj Mahal is considered a well-maintained, high-profit historic asset, not a natural one.)

So how much should a reserve earn, and who's the competition?

Lion destination Kruger National Park in South Africa attracts 1.7 million visitors annually and is reported to support USD 66 billion of wages and salaries (including day and overnight visitors, but apparently not all related revenues) (Wikipedia, Kruger National Park, 2015 figures).

The top-earning national parks in the US earn from USD 179 million to USD 734 million in "visitor spending" annually, per park (the top spot taken by the Great Smoky Mountains National Park), and annual visitors range from 2 million to 9.4 million per park (Explore, 2014). However, the effective revenues should be much more, since only "visitor spending" at the parks is tracked, not related spending in nearby private businesses, such as hotels and restaurants outside the parks (not to mention flights, coach busses, etc.).

Annually, India attracts 11 million foreign visitors and earns USD 30 billion in foreign-exchange revenue from tourism (Wikipedia, Tourism in India, 2019 pre-COVID figures). If just 10% of tourists spent their money in Kanha seeing the iconic tiger, tiger parks would earn **USD 3 billion** (assuming comparable facilities and services to the rest of the nation).

South Africa attracted 8.9 million tourists in the same year as the above park visit figure (Statista, 2023, 2015 figure). If we apply a park tourist rate of 19% (1.7 million park visitors/8.9 million national visitors) to India's tourism revenues (USD 30 billion), then tiger park earnings would be **USD 5.7 billion**.

Perhaps China would be a better comparison country. India and China are both in Asia, both include roughly 1.4 billion citizens, and each offers both historical and tiger tourism. Pre-COVID, China was Asia Pacific's top destination, with nearly 66 million visitors, who spent over USD 40 billion (Wikipedia, World Tourism Rankings, 2019 figures). India was #8 with nearly 18 million visitors, who spent over USD 30 billion. If India attracted the same tourist spending as China, and we assumed that 19% was earned by the parks, tiger earnings would be **USD 7.6 billion** (19% of USD 40 billion) (see Figure 2.1).

Figure 2.1: Tourist getting a close-up shot in the Kanha Nature Reserve.

Is this the actual lower and upper range of target earnings? Probably not, since there are many factors I've not included in my back-of-envelope musings. However, it should make the point that comparisons can be made and targets set to encourage proper management for both protecting our natural assets and using them well to benefit the economy (and all the people in it). We should also investigate the choices tourists make (shall I go to Kruger or Kanha this year?) and why.

So, how much do the tiger parks actually earn?

I don't know.

It may speak to my lack of resourcefulness as a researcher, or it could be that no one tracks those revenues. I've found valuation in terms of the resources held in the parks and found park earnings reported for a selection of parks collectively (e.g., Pench, Kanha, Bandhavgarh, and Panna Nature Reserves together).

However, *I suspect the real answer is that we aren't tracking what we aren't yet managing as a revenue-generating natural asset.*

What was the economic valuation I found of Kanha Nature Reserve? I'll address that below in the section on valuing a tree, tiger, and reserve. For now, suffice it to say that ecological and economic synergy is not only about boosting the economy but also about protecting our ecosystem.

Yes, economic growth is a survival issue for our growing population. But how we power that growth – from clean or dirty energy, producing what sort of waste, and more – is also a survival issue for that growing population. We only have a small window of time in which to clean up our act before we tip the balance of our climate into un-fixable territory.

What Nishi recommended in 2009 to the leaders and managers of the reserves is still a good set of recommendations. We have seen some action on each, and we're watching for more:

- strengthening the management education of those accountable for the performance of these natural assets
- marketing the park as a tourist destination
- creating infrastructure of requisite size and quality to serve tourists with rooms, food, transport, roads, medical facilities, services, souvenirs, etc.
- investing in the population's professional skills, attitudes, and knowledge so they can participate in the economic opportunities created by these investments

What has TTC done to help?
We crafted a new model of conservation which has influenced public policy in the national parliament and various local agencies (described in the Golden Triangle section below). Nishi led the team commissioned by India's Chief Justice to determine the economic value of trees, in order to guide infrastructure decisions (described more fully in its own section below, along with shark, tiger, and reserve valuation).

He's also served as Vice Chairman of the Centre of Science for Villages (CSV), our official partner for the environment, as well as Maharashtra's Ecotourism Development Board, appointed by the leadership of the state. He arranged for community leaders Salim, Mukesh, and Jitesh to go to the CSV and learn first-hand about various ecologically-friendly technologies to adopt in our community, including solar power, biogas, sunbaked air-pocket (thermal) bricks, eco-architectural design, and water harvesting and filtration. We've been encouraging adoption by others and use solar power and water filtration in our vocational schools.

We haven't finished writing and taking action. We just hope our efforts make a difference while we still have natural assets to protect and make productive.

Figure 2.2: Babbar, one of our Royal Bengal Tigers.

Tigers

Traders pay poachers 2,000 rupees (USD 24) for a dead tiger. That's almost half of what a typical farmer makes in a year. The traders can then sell the tiger skin for 50,000 to 80,000 rupees (USD 600 to USD 965), and the bones for up to 120,000 rupees (USD 1,450). Such tiger poaching is one of the gravest threats facing wild tigers today . . . Nowadays, it's estimated that one tiger is poached in India every day.

— Minnesota Zoo (ca. 2004)

Once, over 100,000 of these magnificent cats roamed the Earth. Now only 4,500–6,000 remain (WWF, 2023; higher estimate from the Forest Department of Madhya Pradesh, including 2-year-old and younger tigers, personal communication, 2023) (see Figure 2.2).

Of the tiger's 9 subspecies, 3 are now extinct, and one is functionally extinct (WWF, 2023). Only 5 remain.

About 93% of the tiger's historic habitat has disappeared, or it has emptied due to poaching, depletion of prey along the food chain, and habitat loss affecting tiger prey (Vaidyanathan, 2019).

Approximately 70% of the global tiger population can be found in India (Ministry of Environment, 2016), making wise policy and effective stewardship in India essential to the preservation of the species overall.

Why preserve the tiger? Beyond the tiger's remarkable beauty, as an apex predator, it is a fairly good barometer of the health of its ecosystem. If the forest vegetation isn't healthy, grazing mammals won't be healthy, and they won't be good food for this premier cat.

> If there is no forest, then the tiger gets killed; if there is no tiger, then the forest gets destroyed. Hence, the tiger protects the forest and the forest guards the tiger! *Mahabharat* (Kumbhaghonam Edition) — Udyoga Parva: 5.29.57

Does that have anything to do with humans?

Yes.

Nations that neglect their natural environment are at risk for increased frequency and magnitude of natural disasters – floods, droughts, landslides, earthquakes, and more.

The tiger is worthy of preservation in and of its own right. Beyond that, and beyond acting as an eco-barometer, it is an excellent spokesman for the environment and substantially boosts the economy through tourism.

A nation can follow two basic approaches to protecting a species – (1) direct intervention and (2) protecting its environment so it can flourish on its own. India, through Project Tiger, has taken the second approach, although of necessity, it must also provide forest guards for tigers and their habitat.

Has it worked?

In 1972, Indira Gandhi championed the cause of the tiger and oversaw India's first official (government) tiger census. The results showed a devastating drop from a global population of 100,000 in 1900 to only 2,610–1,827 in India.

She launched Project Tiger with 9 new nature reserves. Villages located within the reserve borders were given incentives to relocate, and a Special Tiger Protection Force (STPF) was launched, alongside other initiatives.

Sadly, official census figures show a *decrease* in tigers to 1,411 in India in 2008, although numbers subsequently increased. The population did not exceed its 1972 level until 2014. Reasons have not been shared, and we can only speculate about disgruntled people who did not want to move from their land, or other conflicts with tigers, e.g., farmers who lose an ox and cannot plant their one crop a year without it.

Tiger–human conflict arises not only from livestock attacks. Between 2015 and 2019, tigers killed 24 people in Chandrapur alone. In the same period, villagers across central India killed 21 tigers via electrocution, poisoning, and traps (Vaidyanathan, 2019). Conservation reports suggest that non-reserve tigers (they are not fenced into the reserves) hunt over longer distances each day, due to depleted game, infrastructure blockages (e.g., roads built without "green corridors"), and to avoid humans. They need 22% more food where it has already grown scarcer. In one study, four non-reserve tigers died by walking into electric wires (which may have been installed for unrelated reasons).

Whether human–tiger conflict caused the census decline or not, managing human–tiger relations will be key to future survival – for them both.

Since that time, we've seen overall numbers rise, amid growing efforts to reduce human–tiger conflict, as well as growing investments in tiger reserves.

Today, there are 54 tiger reserves maintained by the National Tiger Conservation Authority (NTCA) (Dasgupta, 2023), covering over 75,000 sq km (29,000 sq mi) across 18 states (Economic Times, 2022). The official budget for tiger conservation increased from USD 22 million in 2014 to USD 36 million in 2022 (Economic Times, 2022).

Not only have the reserves been established, but they're popularized in the media, and conservation of tigers and their habitat is regularly featured in the media locally, nationally, and internationally. To raise awareness of tiger conservation and promote initiatives for protecting its habitats, for example, Global Tiger Day (July 29) was launched in 2010 at the Saint Petersburg Tiger Summit in Russia. India's prime minister takes part each year in a variety of ways such as hosting awareness campaigns, conferences, speeches, etc.

However, are such events really raising the awareness of the *local* people who live among tigers and reserves? Are the campaigns sharing with *them* the mind-boggling figures and listing the benefits tigers and reserves provide? If they haven't already adopted them, perhaps the same measures companies and political parties use to track marketing campaign effectiveness could help policymakers ensure their conservation campaign resources are used wisely and that the people who can guard these resources are made aware of the need for them to do so.

Is local awareness and guardianship important?

Yes.

When we first approached the Madhya Pradesh Forest Department to ask how we might help them safeguard the tiger and preserve its habitat, they told us they have sufficient guards, training, and guns, but what they want is more community involvement.

Why?

In any rural area, the community is the most effective police force and a crucial investigative resource. Officials are too few and distances too far to be otherwise. There's no way for a few guards overseeing a large forest (in Kanha's case, 940 sq km) to monitor all places at once and arrive on scene quickly enough 100% of the time to prevent poaching or at least catch the poachers in the act. Once poaching has occurred, officials conduct interviews – again, with the community – to gather information for suspect tracking, arrest, and prosecution.

The Sariska tragedy is a case in point. In an effort to gather information from a broader array of forestry officials than our own on the state of operations and what would help them protect the tiger and habitat, we scheduled meetings at the Sariska Tiger Reserve in Rajasthan. When we arrived, we were informed that all meetings were canceled, as there was an emergency.

What was the crisis?

All tigers had been removed from the Sariska Tiger Reserve seemingly overnight.

Officials followed up with people in the community and were told no one saw or heard anything suspicious.

> The nice thing about living in a small town is that when you don't know what you're doing, someone else does. — Immanuel Kant

I can't say I've ever lived in a small town or village (not one of which I spoke the language), so I cannot attest to how much everyone knows of everyone else's business. I also haven't found research that solidly proves small communities know everyone's business.

However, even if we remove that from consideration, where would poachers have gotten food, water, and other supplies? Didn't *anyone* see strangers enter the community? Wouldn't they have spoken to *someone* asking for the whereabouts of tigers within the reserve or at least tiger prey?

It seems unlikely no one noticed strangers in town (or nearby) consuming resources and asking questions.

In our own community, TTC has worked to encourage tiger and cultural tourism (enhancing the community's livelihood) and to provide much-needed medical care and education. Our community knows our message of ecologically- and socially-sensitive economic growth and that The Tiger Center provides essential help.

To reduce human–tiger conflict, we also began providing interim funding to farmers whose livestock had been injured or killed by tigers. The government reimburses them after claims are verified, but they may not happen in time to get a farmer's one crop a year (rice) planted. If one ox is injured or dead, the other cannot pull the plow alone. Interim financing can save a year of lost income – of grave importance to a poor family.

We also introduced beekeeping so people could produce their own honey without going into the forest. When gathering firewood, honey, and tall grass for livestock, people sometimes startle a resting tiger – with dire consequences.

We're fortunate to work in a community with traditional values of harmony with nature, including the Baiga and Gond tribes, as well as the villager-farmers who take from the soil and sell in the marketplace but do not deplete their soil or use excessive pesticides. We enhance and aim to secure what they already know and do.

Early on, we worked closely with the legendary Manglu Baiga, elder of the Baiga tribe, who co-founded the Kanha Nature Reserve. (He has since passed away.) Someone asked him if we could relocate some Kanha tigers to Sariska, since our population is quite healthy and theirs had disappeared.

He replied instantly – no need to consider:

> No. You cannot move our tigers to Sariska. If they can't take care of their own, they can't have ours. — Manglu Baiga, tribal elder and legendary naturalist

In short, awareness is important. Reducing human–tiger conflict is important. However, we need to push further, towards giving humans a reason to protect the tiger and its habitat, as well as ways to survive without encroaching on its environment for firewood, fodder, honey, and other essentials. We're working to improve economic and social-service benefits to humans based on the tiger's presence and a thriving habitat.

In our case, it seems to be working.

Other organizations have followed our lead, ensuring that people who live with the tiger have a reason to protect it – not just sentimental, but solid social and economic benefits they do not want to lose. Some conservation initiatives, for example, set aside social service and economic development funding as part of conservation budgets. Tigers and people both benefit, and the benefits to one reinforce the other.

Although the tiger population is growing, securing its future is far from certain. In some places (including much of Southeast Asia), the population is still declining (WWF, 2023).

Perhaps an integrated approach to ecological, social, and economic development would help. We can at least begin with solid analysis – of (1) the economic potential of our ecology and (2) the ecological impact of our economy.

Figure 2.3: Tiger (lower left), at one with his environment.

What's a Shark Worth – or a Tree, Tiger, or Tiger Reserve?

> There is no point of contact between macroeconomics and the environment.
> — Herman Daly, World Bank economist

Beyond the above, are there other economic–ecological analyses that connect macroeconomics and the environment?

Yes.

A study on sharks in Palau, for example, (Australian Institute of Marine Scientists, as referenced in Yale School of the Environment, 2011) showed that each shark attracted USD 179,000 a year in ecotourist revenues – USD 1.9 million during its lifetime.

Compare that with the price of a dead shark (on its way to being fish and chips): USD 200.

A shark fin: USD 108.

Shark fin nutritional value: 0.

Shark fin status value: once high but now endangered, thanks to Asia's courageous younger generations, who increasingly refuse to serve it at weddings and other traditional occasions.

Sadly, WWF (2023) estimates that nearly 30% of the 1,000+ shark species are "at risk" of extinction, due to overfishing (including finning), habitat loss, and climate change.

What can we do? Palau established itself as a shark sanctuary (yes, the entire nation) and Guam, Hawaii, the Marshall Islands, and the Northern Marianas followed suit.

Do sharks serve as a good analogy for tigers? Perhaps. Before examining tiger economics, however, let's look at a key part of its habitat: the tree (see Figure 2.3).

When approving or denying proposals for roadways and other infrastructure, the government of India requires an Environmental Impact Assessment. The timber value of trees has traditionally been the arboreal measure of choice. However, India's Chief Justice recognized its inadequacy.

> Why do authorities, while computing environmental compensation, not take into account the volume of oxygen a tree would release into the atmosphere in its lifetime? — Chief Justice of India, Sharad Bobde (Mahapatra, 2020)

A 2020 court case brought the issue clearly into the media spotlight when a decision had to be made to allow or forbid cutting 356 heritage trees (80+ years old) to construct five railway over-bridges.

> According to scientists, global warming will lead to increase of temperature by seven degrees Celsius in 50 years, which will wipe out the human race on earth. Trees and increase in green cover are the only means to combat global warming. The state government must consider alternatives, including underpasses [, existing waterways and railway lines,] and changing alignment of roads, to avoid felling of precious heritage trees. — Prashant Bhushan, Advocate in the "Heritage Trees Case" (Mahapatra, 2020)

The Supreme Court commissioned a panel (led by TTC Managing Director Prof. Nishikant Mukerji) to examine the issues. They concluded that the value of a tree is its age multiplied by INR 74,500 (USD 911) (Anand, 2021).

For the first time in India, this established the value of a tree in both fully economic *and* ecological terms and provided a valid measure with which to guide policymakers' infrastructure and development decisions. The panel added that a heritage tree aged 100+ could be valued at more than INR 10 million (USD 122,000).

Just over 60% of the new valuation is oxygen, 27% biofertilizers, and 13% micronutrients and compost. The panel added that most upcoming projects will not be worth as much as the new valuation of the trees in question.

If trees must be removed, the committee proposed that decision-makers first consider using modern technology to relocate trees without harming them. If that is infeasible, the panel advised that planting 5 new trees for each one felled (an earlier practice) is not sufficient to replace the ecological services of a mature tree. Members proposed replacement of 10 saplings for mature trees with a small crown size, 25 for medium, and 50 for large.

The supreme court bench also called untenable the motion to eliminate the Environmental Impact Assessment (EIA) requirement for proposed roadways less than 100 kilometers (62 miles).

The 356 heritage trees remain standing, and the EIA remains both a wise practice and a legal requirement.

Beyond the valuation of sharks and trees, can we estimate economically what a tiger is worth?

Yes.

According to Verma et al. (2017), each tiger provides annual benefits of USD 2.2 million.

How about reserves?

When scientists analyzed six tiger reserves collectively, they estimated the secure-capital value of the reserves at INR 230 billion (USD 2.8 billion). Annual maintenance cost (all six reserves studied): USD 2.8 million.

Return on Investment: 35,600%. (No, that's not a typo.)

In Verma et al.'s 2019 study of 10 reserves, they found annual direct returns ranged from USD 616 million–2 billion. Beyond the numbers, they noted that the reserves offer climate change resilience and potential for groundbreaking scientific discoveries in biomimicry, crop resilience, pharmaceuticals, and more. Options valuation (which originated in the financial services industry for derivatives pricing) could offer an approach for further valuation – and support for preservation.

Perhaps their most significant (and memorable) finding was that every dollar invested in the studied reserves yielded a return of USD 30.

That's right – the reserves transformed USD 1 into USD 30.

Collectively, for just these 10 reserves, the ecosystem services both directly and indirectly impacting the local population were valued at USD 1.3–4.2 billion per year, including:

- USD 200–852 million of resources
- USD 310–999 million of ecosystem services (e.g., maintaining a benign physical and chemical environment for humans)

– up to USD 7.5 million of recreational and socio-cultural benefits (the values
   and cultural traditions of the local community are rooted in the reserves and
   their tigers)
– USD 4 million provision of water
– USD 931,000–USD 2.9 million of protection from diseases, parasites, and
   predators

Additional tangible and intangible flow benefits included biological control, climate regulation, cultural heritage, carbon sequestration, employment generation,
fishing, fodder, fuelwood, gas regulation, gene pool protection, moderation of ex-
treme events, nutrient retention, pollination, sediment retention/soil conservation, and spiritual tourism.

Is there a valuation of a single reserve?

Yes.

One study of the Kanha Nature Reserve estimated ecosystem benefits at INR
16.5 billion annually (USD 199 million), including (Wikipedia, Kanha Tiger Reserve, n.d.).:

– USD 150 million for gene-pool protection
– USD 2.6 million for carbon sequestration
– USD 6.7 million for downstream water provisioning
– USD 6.6 million for livestock fodder in buffer areas
– USD 4.6 million for recreation
– USD 3.8 million for wildlife habitat

According to Secretary General of the Global Tiger Forum Rajesh Gopal, over the
last 35 years, the Indian government has spent USD 180 million on tiger conservation and received over USD 23 billion per year from just 6 reserves (*Hindustan
Times*, 2017).

> This new way of green accounting is seldom considered by traditional economists. — Rajesh
> Gopal, Secretary General of the Global Tiger Forum, New Delhi (Verma et al., 2017)

It would seem that green accounting has made significant contributions so far
and should grow further, enabling us to make better, more integrated decisions.

Now we just have to use it.

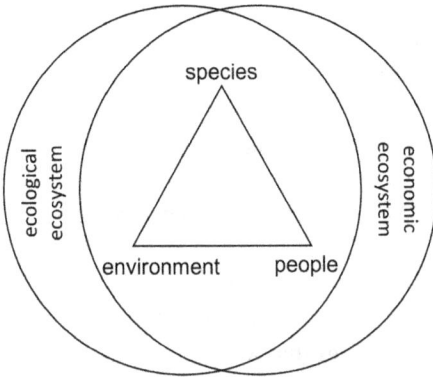

Figure 2.4: The Tiger Center's Golden Triangle Model of Conservation.

The Golden Triangle Model of Conservation

> The ecological perspective . . . cannot treat the earth as something separate from human civilization . . . we are, in effect, a natural force just like the winds and the tides.
> — Al Gore

The Tiger Center's "Golden Triangle" model of conservation (see Figure 2.4) has been discussed in the Parliament of India and impacted public policy in the areas of forestry and reserves. In Kanha, for example, after years of extolling the beauty of the reserve during rainy season and the market potential for a 12-month tourist year (instead of 9 months), reserve policy was amended to allow tourists into the buffer zone of Kanha-Kisli year round.

New roads were built from Mansar to Khawasa with wildlife corridors built in. A new reserve zone and gate (Khatiya) was opened to serve the increased flow of tourists, and a community water reservoir was placed nearby (which also attracts wildlife towards the reserve entrance). It could have been placed anywhere, but this location enhances "customer experience." Further, some government agencies have expanded their tiger focus (and budgets) to include initiatives for the environment and local people.

What is the "Golden Triangle" model and how is it different? Very simply, it is an approach that integrates the needs of endangered species (in this case, the tiger), the environment (for us, the Kanha Nature Reserve), and the people who live alongside both (in our case, Baiga and Gond tribes, as well as villagers).

Traditional conservation is concerned with species and habitats – not with people.

To save an endangered species, you must save both it and its natural habitat, so it can live naturally and (hopefully) thrive well enough to no longer be threatened with extinction. The best guardians of the forest (who can also be the most damaging invaders) are the people who live alongside both. They need to have a reason to protect species and environment (and not encroach).

Normally, this will be in the form of:

- **sustenance**, e.g., earning a living through ecotourism or habitat-independent means
- **services** connected to the species – in our case, medical care, education, and other services given by The Tiger Center, obviously connected to the tiger
- **strengthening and sharing of cultural values** that we must live in harmony with our wildlife and environment, in our case, the traditional values held by Baigas and Gonds, as well as the values held by the villagers and TTC's international leaders

If the species has nowhere to live, it won't thrive.

If the environment cannot thrive, it cannot support species or people.

If the local people cannot thrive, it only takes one to endanger the species and environment. Just one person can strike a match that "clears land for farming" but destroys vast natural spaces – or set traps and invite poachers.

If one is to survive and thrive, all three must do so.

As you can see from the discussions above and elsewhere on ecology's impact on the economy (generally positive) and the economy's impact on ecology (generally negative), the two overlap and are currently out of balance (positive flows to economy but negative to ecology).

Beyond the challenge of helping all three thrive, there is another challenge – a dual challenge:

- optimize value for both economy and ecology where they overlap, and
- minimize negative impact of each on the other, where there is no overlap

In short, positive value investments and initiatives like those discussed above should grow, and green accounting should guide us as to how far to grow them so we don't eventually encounter negative marginal returns.

On the edges – where ecology and economy do not overlap – choices sit in their own space but must be kept "eco-impact-neutral" (both "ecos" – ecology and economy). It doesn't matter to the environment whether we produce white or black electronic vehicles – unless, of course, one or the other wastes energy by requiring more heating or cooling, or if one paint color is toxic. Likewise, it doesn't matter to the economy whether a water catchment area is placed here or there – unless, of course, it is placed in a location that boosts ecotourism.

Ecological and economic spheres have both been labeled with the term "eco-system," because, in fact, each operates in an ecosystem, and all stakeholders of that ecosystem will have to operate in harmony not only with their own sphere, but also with the other. Business, government, academe, and community stake-holders must all operate together. It only takes one ecologically-extreme group to disrupt business with a media event or asset damage, and it only takes one busi-ness to disrupt ecology with toxic waste or spillage. Government agencies do not always work in concert when seen from the ground up, and although academics do build on each other's work to create a useful body of evidence, collaboration can also dissolve into factional fighting and research defense through focus on less-than-useful minutiae.

There's another important element necessary for a living ecosystem – the ability to change. For the environment, we call it decomposition and growth. For an economy or social system, we call it creative destruction (or dissent) and co-creation for growth.

Whatever we devise to manage our ecosystems will, in essence, be a meta-ecosystem. I look forward to seeing robust strategies, structures, and systems in our organizations going forward that will serve all stakeholders well, foster wise decisions through green accounting, and last as long as we have ecologies and economies to protect and grow.

Chapter 3
Profit (and Not-for-Profit)

> If we cannot make a profit, that means we are
> committing a sort of crime against society. We take
> society's capital, we take their people, we take their
> materials, yet without a good profit, we are using
> precious resources that could be better used
> elsewhere.
> — Konosuke Matsushita, founder of Matsushita
> Electric Industrial Co., which later became Panasonic
> Holdings Corporation

Do profits and stewardship belong in a discussion of environment and society?

Yes. All capital – natural and economic (traditionally economic) – is subject to the same principles of stewardship.

Profit is not the same as profiteering, and good stewardship includes both capital protection and productivity.

Profit should be approached carefully, like the tiger it is (or can be) so it doesn't become a goal in and of itself or the only goal we work for. The mission is why we're working, and well-chosen measures help drive our behavior in a positive direction. Profit is an important measure, but it's not the only one.

Visionary entrepreneurs and leaders do not seek merely to grab as much money as possible and stuff it in their pockets. That's the job of a bank robber. (So, make sure you're applying for the right job.)

Good leaders seek to create big value – usually for multiple stakeholders – and keep a portion for themselves. How much is reasonable to keep is a debate for another day, and every economic system and faith sets its own standards for ownership and sharing.

That said, I don't know any economy or faith that says it's bad to create more with what you've been given.

In short, stewardship is the game, not profiteering.

Total value created is the end goal, with wins for everyone (environment included, so include it in your stakeholder analysis) – including the leader and his/her organization.

That's not an easy job.

Since done well, it is a difficult job that can create much good, I've always taken exception to the idea that making profits is unreasonably selfish or inappropriate to environmental or social work. It's just a measure of success and

https://doi.org/10.1515/9783110783179-003

doesn't happen if you're creating less value for others than you do for yourself. Seen in this way, profits are inherently unselfish.

Again, profits only happen (and happen sustainably) when you create more for others than you keep.

I've heard leaders of other organizations insist that they and none of their workers should be paid, and all of their administrative necessities should be donated. However, if only the wealthy can engage in environmental or social work, then it becomes a hobby for the rich, not value-creating work (and a source of needed income) for everyone.

I think it's more important to include everyone.

In fact, if it were wrong to engage in profit-making, why would we conduct programs to help people earn a living and encourage base-of-pyramid micro-entrepreneurship?

So, profitability and stewardship are appropriate topics for species, environment, and people, and key questions include:

– How shall we protect our resources and create value with them?
– How shall we establish measures of success to guide our behavior?
– What shall we do with our resources, including stakeholder sharing?

Protection of species and environment is addressed above, including economic benefits from using them productively. Green accounting and triple-bottom-line management offer ways to measure and set goals. Sizable literatures on these topics are widely available.

This chapter is about the third question and what one organization decided to do with:

– the land the leaders believed was God-given,
– diverse social connections and the talents they brought in, and
– both time and money as they became available.

It all started with a late-night conversation . . .

When Men Dream Dreams Over Wine Late at Night

The second step in The Tiger Center story (after the initial purchase of high-potential land) is actually the idea generation phase and a family story. My husband (Chris Marshall) and brother (Nishi Mukerji) were having wine one night while I was diapering babies (yes, I'm a businessperson and a mom).

The 2004 Indian Ocean earthquake and tsunami had just occurred, with a magnitude of 9.1–9.3 – the third-largest earthquake ever recorded and the largest in the 21st century (6.3 is considered strong). The epicenter was just off Aceh, Indonesia (the northwest coast of Sumatra), which is about 1,300 km (800 mi) from Singapore (about 2 hours 45 minutes if you were to fly directly there).

Waves were up to 30 meters high (100 feet). Nearly 230,000 people across 14 countries died. It was one of the deadliest natural disasters in recorded history.

We discussed how we're seeing larger, more widespread natural disasters ever more frequently. Simultaneously, mankind is captivated with making life better, while ignoring the environment – or worse, taking advantage of it economically without protecting, restoring, or enhancing it.

Chris and Nishi continued talking and dreamed dreams of taking action – very sensible ones, as it turned out – focused on one way they could make a difference. They wanted to use the land Nishi had bought wisely and make a broader impact with whatever they did. Ideas included:

- somehow helping tiger conservation (we didn't yet know how),
- developing an eco-sensitive resort to boost the economy and spread awareness of the tiger and its habitat,
- establishing a corporate education center for environmentally-sound business practices (which was put on hold as our mission evolved, but hasn't disappeared altogether),
- influencing government policy with whitepapers and speaking engagements, and
- providing some sort of assistance to the community, since some of the world's poorest people live here.

They agreed that what we do should have local impact and global influence (leading to more impact). They also agreed I should lead it, since my husband's strengths lie in concepts and analysis, my brother's in advising chairmen and CEOs, and mine in both strategy and execution (as a former corporate strategist and current entrepreneur).

I had no idea how things would turn out – or how to say no.

I would find out (but never could say no).

Figure 3.1: Munna, one of our most famous tigers.

Tiger as Spokesman (OK, Spokestiger)

> An animal's eyes have the power to speak a great
> language.
> — Martin Buber

The first thing I knew was that the tiger is charismatic – a great spokesman for its species, habitat, and any business that would work for them. The Tiger Center seemed an obvious name, and the domain (tigercenter.org) was available. My brother had taken a beautiful photo of a tiger walking towards the camera, and we chose him as our "spokestiger." (He's on the cover of this book.)

It wasn't until years later that the "CAT PM" tiger (see Figure 3.1) walked our way and was captured in a photograph. It took a while to realize, but the natural markings on his forehead (in the photo, opposite) actually spell "CAT PM," suggesting that he's the Prime Minister of Tigers. (No, the photo is not Photoshopped.)

We also didn't know that tigers would grow so plentiful in our reserve that the government would eventually open a retirement area for the older ones who couldn't fight the young for territory. Munna safely retired and passed away from old age.

In discussions over what really underlies our desires and goals and what common threads run through them, we came to a simple mission statement that has served us well for nearly two decades:

Help the Tiger, Help the Environment, Help the People

It's simple enough that everyone we work with knows and remembers it – team members and broader community – and it focuses our efforts on the Golden Triangle.

Business Model Transition: From Operators to Partners

The one thing I insisted on at the outset was that it had to be self-supporting. All the co-founders were already major charity donors, and I had heard too many complaints from charity leaders of donor dropouts and economic crises that spurred donation-cutting as businesses' first line of defense. I couldn't set us up to begin offering essential services, then closing down the first time a crisis hit.

Not only did we need to meet a sustainability mission, but we needed to operate sustainably.

The most obvious cash-generation engine was the resort, followed by "green" executive education, which could be held in the resort during off-season and then move to its own facility if and when it grew large enough to do so. Grass-roots efforts in micro-entrepreneurship partnerships (e.g., crafts, organic vegetables for the resort, and services for tourists) could also follow, but would not provide the level of support a resort could. So, a portion of profits from the resort plus corporate (and other) donations were targeted as the inflow to support whatever operations we would devise.

Nishi recruited a team of busy professionals (all friends and long-time associates) to graciously volunteer. Given time zones and time constraints, it took a surprisingly long time to get a budget together for resort development and operations. I realized that although the team included a 5-star hotel head of strategy, a 5-star hotel chef, a corporate strategist, an architect, local entrepreneurs (who could source people and materials), and more, we didn't have anyone with hotel/resort *operations* experience, and it would be a long time before we could support our own full-time staff.

Over time, it became clear that we really should change the business model from owner-operator to lessor-partner, i.e., the resort should be built and operated by a partner who leased the land – someone already in the business, with an existing customer base, operations protocols, supply chain, and more. Why reinvent the wheel?

Research followed to identify all the top corporate resort developers and operators, as well as any private developer/operators. I learned a lot contacting every major hotel chain (and some private ones) across the world.

First, the major chains generally do not develop – they operate. Building a hotel is most commonly an owner/investor activity. Second, they don't want small, boutique properties. They make money with scale.

When I had one business left on my list (others have approached us since then), I was largely ready to give up. I contacted the CEO (or his office – I don't remember) and politely shared the information on what we wanted to do.

To my utter amazement (yes, I was tired and discouraged after chasing all the wrong leads), someone contacted us back. An executive from that company would come visit us and report back to the CEO with facts, photos, videos, and his own personal impressions.

I had no idea at the time that I had worked my way through all the wrong partners and found the best in the business (at least, for our vision) and one of the top-earning and most eco-sensitive in the world.

Next came a question: should we remain one integrated organization for all the activities we envisioned? As it turned out, no. We wound up separating our profit-making family business activities from our not-for-profit pursuits, although keeping them coupled so the business could provide steady support (a portion of profits) to what would remain in The Tiger Center.

In fact, I would later learn that this business model – coupling a profit-making entity with a not-for-profit entity – was a key structure instituted by the Tatas and Birlas from their business beginnings. As the business grew, so would the foundation (or other form of NPO), and the foundation would keep leaders grounded and everyone inspired that their work not only creates marketplace but also societal value. In our family's case, we find the Christian practice of tithing keeps us focused not only on creating marketplace good but on growing the value we devote to people, profit, and planet.

How Corporate Social Responsibility (CSR) Really Works

So, while chasing the profit side of the organization, I also chased the donation side. Again, I made a list of the world's top organizations that seemed suited to our mission and situation and started connecting.

One by one (although it felt like it was in lumps and droves), they turned us down. Why? We didn't operate in their location; we weren't relevant to their business; we hadn't been in operation long enough; and the list went on.

Basically, what I learned about corporate social responsibility (CSR – business-funded charitable activities or donations) is that quite often, it's a value-added business activity – and rightly so. If a company runs social programs in the communities where they operate, they create goodwill among employees (and potential ones), customers (and potential ones), and community. Remember, as mentioned above, community can be the best rural police force or at least a socio-political force to reckon with.

Although many businesses do CSR activities unrelated to their business, it makes sense to seek tighter collaboration between the two. For example, data philanthropy has become a force for good. Companies with data on food supply and distribution networks can donate what they know in a crisis (e.g., earthquake, hurricane, flood, etc.) to efficiently get supplies where they're needed most. (If they have distribution facilities or partners, all the better. They can put those to use, too.)

We did fly to a large foundation to give a presentation and discuss potential support. They didn't extend support (requiring a minimum of 5 years of operations, which we didn't yet have), but they did give us some very good advice on whether to call ourselves a charity or a not-for-profit (we hadn't worked out our language or form of business yet) and which form to register ourselves as with the government.

New Model: From Charity/NGO/NPO to Social Enterprise (+ESG)

If we had registered as a charity, all we could do commercially would be to take donations (at least, in our jurisdiction). If we registered as an NPO, we could raise money in a variety of ways, including donations, services, sale of products from microentrepreneurial programs, and much more.

What's the difference between an NGO and an NPO? Basically none, although NGOs often deal with global/widespread issues, whereas NPOs focus on local action (sometimes scalable worldwide).

Given the restriction on charity revenues and their often inherent instability (due to reliance on donors), we registered as a "Section 25 corporation" – an NPO.

It seems odd to me to define an organization by what it's "not," but perhaps it points to the fact that these organizations operate in a gray area not covered by business or government. They can also serve as a catalyst for business-government cooperation precisely because they operate in the gray.

As we grew and shared our vision with others, we discovered a new form of business (or at least a new name) – the social enterprise.

A "social enterprise" applies business strategy to create maximum value in economic, environmental, and social terms (Wikipedia, Social Enterprise). Legal forms of social enterprise (depending on jurisdiction) can include not-for-profit (which may prohibit profit distribution to owners), limited corporation, partnership, co-operative, mutual organization, and more. Profits are generally reinvested in its programs to achieve an environmental and/or social mission.

How is social enterprise different from a "triple bottom line" organization? The triple bottom line approach extends the success measures for a traditional (profit-making) business to include people and planet. A social enterprise, on the other hand, includes people and/or planet as primary elements of its mission.

How is social enterprise different from CSR? Most companies have added CSR onto the existing business and report CSR activities separately from the key financial results of the company. For a social enterprise, "CSR" results are the key results, since they are central to the mission.

How is social enterprise different from environment, social, and (corporate) governance (ESG)? ESG's primary focus is to monitor a company's activities in terms of sustainability – environmental, social, and governance – addressing issues such as climate change risk, employee diversity, corporate board and management structures, etc.

ESG is about how you operate. Social enterprise is about the mission.

In fact, they go together quite well, since a social enterprise needs to operate sustainably, like any other.

How?

Although environment and social issues are part of a social enterprise's mission, it also needs to ensure that its operations are sustainable. It would be inappropriate, for example, for an environmental activist group to waste (or improperly dispose of) paper, plastic, and other materials in the course of its work. In the area of social sustainability, it would seem odd if an enterprise created to help women were staffed entirely by men – or worse yet, only men at the leadership level. Equally, in the area of governance, no donor wants to find out that their hard-earned money has been wasted by corruption, excessive executive compensation, poor tax planning and execution, or inaccurate/incomplete accounting records reported without transparency.

Bottom line: TTC is a social enterprise, registered as an NPO, and managed sensitively towards ESG, albeit without a formal ESG team (which we may develop after further growth). We are affiliated with a family business (resort), which will be a regular donor, to be joined by others as we expand our CSR donor base and activities.

Figure 3.2: Tiger-viewing from jeep or elephant – a unique offering.

The Longest Contract Negotiations in History

> Let us not grow weary of doing good, for in due
> season we will reap, if we do not give up.
> — New International Version Bible, 1984,
> Galatians 6:9

Resort partner negotiations have taken 15 years (so far) – longer than many partnerships last!

What happened?

After our potential partner's executive returned to the office, he reported that the opportunity was excellent and worth seeing. Kanha was (at the time) the only place in the world to see tigers from jeep and elephant (see Figure 3.2), and certainly the only place to see at least one tiger a day (in the wild). (The elephant viewing has since ceased, because it's now so easy to view tigers from jeep roadways. However, viewing from elephant is a special experience, and we are encouraging the forest department to re-launch.)

So the founder and CEO came. Here, I'll call him Mr. Legend, since he's a legend in the hospitality industry.

Within 45 minutes of his scheduled arrival time, Legend saw his first tiger.

Afterwards, he walked the land, examined many things, asked lots of questions, and summed up his assessment in one word.

"Spectacular!"

This greatly warmed our hearts and kept them warm during the ensuing contract negotiations. Since we're such a good fit in terms of the product/service to be offered (common design sensibilities), environmental sensitivity, community impact, and management style, negotiations went well, and we agreed on terms. We would lease the land, and Legend's company would build and operate.

He would present plans to the board for approval (a mere formality) on October 2, 2008.

On September 29, the stock market crashed.

The global economic crisis of 2008 had begun.

The board had to deny – for the first time – Legend's project. They also had to stop all development projects, since banks (with whom they had contracts for financing) had no money.

Unbelievable. Banks had no money.

Less than a year earlier, Legend had sold his company for USD 400 million to a big developer to gain access to large amounts of capital with which to expand his highly-successful resort business. The developer had bought the company to serve as a "jewel in its crown," boosting its brand as one of quality and style.

The quality and style lasted. The capital did not.

The big developer lost USD 900 million of its USD 1 billion stock market valuation overnight.

It had to sell, or it would go bankrupt.

And so the sale process began. First one, then another potential buyer approached, and negotiations broke down each time for various reasons. The developer appointed Goldman Sachs as an advisor to help.

Was there anything we could do to develop a new resort during this time with Legend or his company? No, not really.

We did investigate another partner, but they ignored our advice that ours is the best location. We shared the problems they would face with other locations, but they put their resort elsewhere. Once open for business, customers complained of noisy buses and trucks awakening them at odd hours, the hour-long journey through the reserve to get to plentiful wildlife, and more. The business didn't do very well.

We also considered yet another partner, but our design sensibilities, eco-sensitivity, and management style were not a good fit. On their own, they began construction of a resort near the reserve. They blocked the waterway to subsistence-farmers downstream in order to create a water feature for high-end guests.

The farmers didn't appreciate it.

When informed of the problem, the company representative declared it their right to do so.

Mysteriously, their project office building burned down, and a note was found saying if they didn't leave, worse would happen. Remember: local community can make or break a rural business.

They left.

They bought land at another location, perhaps hoping the forestry service would open another gate nearby. That hasn't happened, and guests face a long drive to locations of plentiful wildlife.

After nearly seven years, Legend and a joint venture partner bought back his company (minus one hotel) for USD 358 million.

Hurrah! The company was back in its founder's capable hands, and we could partner for growth, right?

Not yet.

Shortly after the transaction, disagreement arose as to who controlled the company, and the dispute eventually wound up in court.

After years of disagreements, Legend left.

He started a new brand in a part of the market he was told couldn't support his type of offering. As with the first company, which upturned the industry's business model and assumptions, the new company would do the same.

The following year, he came again, saw the land, visited community members, and met with us. He had a backlog of projects to launch, since so much time had been eaten up in disagreements at the old company. When our turn came, we were ready to get moving.

Then COVID struck.

That was not the time to arrange funding for travel-related projects or to invite an international team (development executive, architect, on-site development manager, etc.) to travel to a new project site or to ship building supplies from overseas. We would have to wait.

Now, the pandemic has finished, and we're seeing pent-up demand for travel and wellness (green) destinations. We've signed terms (better ones, actually), but not a contract, while some important issues are being worked out. We have no doubt that the God who brought us this far will carry us all the way. We listen for His instructions, do what we can, and keep moving forward.

Our relationship with Legend has remained strong over the years despite all the difficulties, and our values remain the same. Our relationship with him is very precious to us, and we're blessed that he's still as excited about the development vision as we are.

Keep moving forward. — Walt Disney

It's Actually the Team That Leads

Nothing happened the way we planned. The circumstances above blindsided us – and everyone around the world. Not only did global crises derail our plans, but it derailed team members' businesses and jobs. I was no exception.

When the global crisis of 2008 hit, business revenues of every company I had founded on three continents in a variety of industries went to USD 0 overnight. My attention was needed elsewhere, and TTC didn't have a source of income for all we did, either.

I told the team we needed to stop operations while there's no money coming in.

They said no. People depend on us. We'd have to operate with volunteers on a "shoestring" budget provided by themselves and anyone else they could contact.

I applauded them and told them I'd need to step down – they should appoint a new leader.

They said no. I needed to stay put.

Obviously, I have a great deal of influence in the organization.

As it turns out, they were right.

We kept moving and never, never, never, never gave in.

We survived, and so did the people who depend on us.

I'm glad they were right.

Figure 3.3: The hoopoe: a symbol of hope.

Rainbows, Hoopoes, and Hope

> Never, never, never, never give in . . . except to
> convictions of honour and good sense.
> — Winston Churchill

While the team faced difficulties in Kanha, I faced difficulties, too, supporting business and family. Every contract for all our family businesses had to be renegotiated, and almost all employees had to be fired – truly no choice, but relationships were kept, and one later returned from overseas to work with us. I would have to do whatever jobs needed to be done.

The children and I moved overseas, with my husband remaining alone in Asia, and everyone got by one day at a time.

Even when I broke my leg and had no insurance or money for healthcare, I did get by each day of the 6 months it took to heal. I developed greater sympathy than ever before for people without healthcare. I was without a doctor, too.

In sport science, there's a concept called "dysfunctional overstressing," also called overtraining. Overtaxing a muscle, letting it heal stronger, then overtaxing, in order to heal even stronger, is how we grow stronger. However, if there's never time to heal, and we're only overtaxing, our efforts are only damaging.

Mothers who work both in the marketplace and in the home are particularly prone to overstressing dysfunctionally and burning out. As someone who's done it, I'm aware of the signs and try to encourage my team to train but not overtrain, work for our mission, but not push when it's not working. It may not be time yet. We may need to wait for God or community to align all the pieces that'll make it work.

There's a spirit and flow when things will work that you can't push by yourself.

The above quote from Churchill was a great comfort to me every day. God also sent a surprising series of comforts – rainbows. In the Bible (Genesis 9:13–14), God placed a rainbow in the sky after the great flood as a sign that he would never again send a great flood to destroy life. Many people see it as an everlasting promise of care and protection.

Whenever I was having a particularly hard day or felt exceedingly discouraged, I saw a rainbow – sometimes doubles. They came again and again and again and again. I had never seen so many.

After some time, when our businesses stabilized and life with the kids was more settled, I wondered where the rainbows went. Why didn't I see them anymore?

Most people will tell you it's silly to believe in signs.

But who wants to be most people?

One day when I was on my laptop by the phone doing business things while the kids were in school, I saw a bird I'd never seen in our location before – a hoopoe. I had only seen them in India near our land and had photographed one (see Figure 3.3).

This new hoopoe landed in exactly the same position just outside the window and maintained his (or her) position while I got a good (astonished) look. Again, I felt it was a sign that something good connected to TTC would happen.

I would just have to hold on and be patient.

Creative Conflict and the Whole-Brained Team

After some time, the tension between Nishi, my husband Chris, and I grew intense. We're all creative thinkers who appreciate new concepts/frameworks, strategy, business models, the visual arts, and the future. Connecting with each other based on that (including the TTC mission, vision, and strategy) was easy.

The rest of it got hard.

At one point, Nishi scolded us for being uncaring and not putting the team and community first, in line with our mission. Chris scolded us for doing unproductive things and not having enough impact with thought leadership, which insightful analysis on what we're doing could easily remedy. I scolded everyone for not getting things done. We're building an organization, after all, and need to make it all more than just thinking and words.

Little did we know, that was our strength.

One day, when stewing after yet another disagreement, I remembered something I had taught about teams when delivering corporate executive education.

One of the most important tools I use for individuals and teams (be they start-ups, innovation teams, leadership teams, partnerships, etc.) is the Hermann Brain Dominance Instrument (HBDI®). Based on extensive thinking- and behavioral-style research and Nobel-prize-winning neuroscience, HBDI® characterizes our thinking styles not just as left-brained (logical) or right-brained (creative).

Most of us are:
- left-brained (logical),
- right-brained (creative),
- top-brained (logical and creative thinkers), or
- bottom-brained (doers and feelers).

A small segment of the population is cross-brained. They'll be folks who are:
- logical thinkers (top-left-brained – good with analysis) who are also feelers (bottom-right-brained – creative folks who prioritize emotions), or in the other cross-wise direction
- creative thinkers (top-right-brained – future-oriented folks good with strategy, design, and visuals) who are also logical doers (bottom-left-brained – those who get things done and enjoy checking off a to-do list).

Why were we a good team? Because:
- We were all creative thinkers who could see the TTC vision and were happy to work for its future, developing strategy, design, and more
- Each of us covered another of the three remaining quadrants – analyzing for wise decisions, taking care of team and community, and ensuring things got done.

Why were we fighting?

Same reasons.

Teams need to cover all the "bases," whether startup, innovation, or leadership team, be they social enterprise, traditional business, or hobby club. At the end of the day, "whole-brained" teams are effective, resilient, and crucial for innovation and startup success (Leonard, 1997).

So, I shared this framework with Chris and Nishi, and they agreed that we needed to appreciate each other's differences more while using them productively.

Creative dissonance is good – not destructive, counter-productive dissonance.

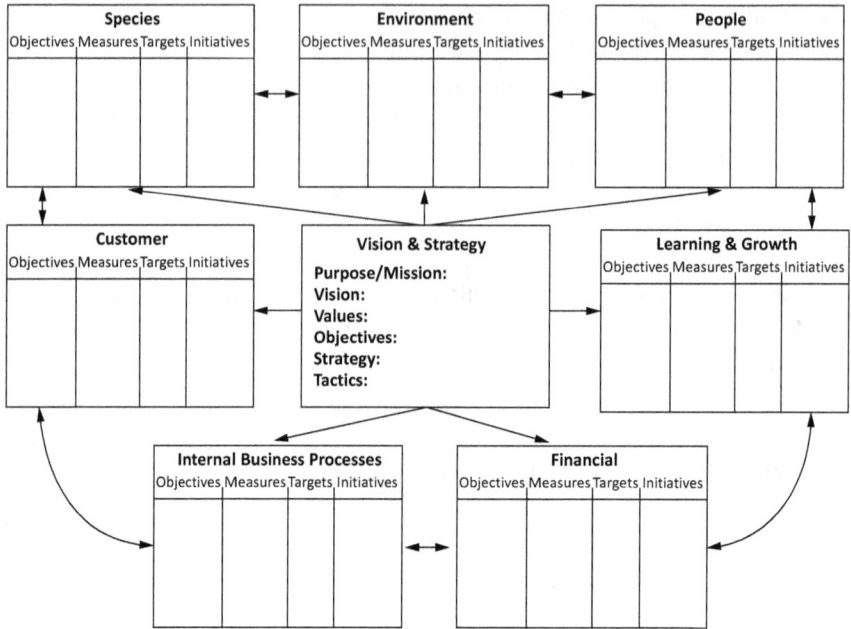

Figure 3.4: The Golden Triangle Balanced Scorecard.

The Golden Triangle Balanced Scorecard

While we're on the topic of management, if an organization other than ours wanted to enact the Golden Triangle, how would they do it organizationally? One approach would be the balanced scorecard (Kaplan and Norton, 1996).

As illustrated in Figure 3.4, the standard balanced scorecard includes a focus on four key areas of any business: customers, internal processes, financial results, and learning and growth initiatives. We've added species, environment, and people at the top to bring them clearly into focus and ensure management attention on them.

Leadership teams normally begin by developing (or reviewing) the vision and strategy of the organization as a whole (in the center of the graphic). They then break out into separate working groups for each box (e.g., customer satisfaction team, operations, finance, innovation, etc.). If a leader/team is in charge of more than one box, no problem, they continue the process with more than one.

Teams responsible for results in each key area determine what their objectives, measures, and targets should be (in line with overall strategy) and decide on initiatives to pursue. They review what they've planned in order to ensure plans are integrated and reasonable, as well as to eliminate inconsistencies. Once the breakout teams are done, the core group reconvenes and reviews the plans, again seeking to ensure integration, reasonableness, and consistency.

Once a quarter (or whenever deemed appropriate), results are tracked against plans. Either plans are revised, or actions are taken to achieve desired results.

The approach can be very useful in uncovering inconsistencies in the whole, imbalances of effort and attention, and disjointed strategy and action. Organizations can, of course, change the boxes as needed for their own type of organization and focus.

We haven't used this approach yet, as it's often best applied to larger organizations. That said, there's no rule that says it can't be used for small ones, too.

If it's useful for your situation, we hope you use it.

Figure 3.5: Serpent eagle drying wings in the Kanha sun.

Words (and Brands) Have Wings

> A brand is a living entity, and it is enriched or
> undermined cumulatively, over time, the product of a
> thousand small gestures.
> — Michael Eisner

We didn't really set out to create a brand, but in the thousand small and large actions we've taken, we've found that we do have a brand, and it stands for integrity, informed action, and empathy for tigers, environment, and people.

We used to approach people and explain who we are and what we do.

Now, people approach us and explain how they'd like to help, what they'd like to see happen, or what they need.

Now that we're known, it is easier to operate and grow, and people are watching like never before that we maintain the trust we've earned. We began communicating with people via the website, Facebook, and group emails, and we find our audience growing without any particular campaign to do so. Some of our audience accesses our online presence, but many more cannot, and our messages are carried by word of mouth.

The brand itself has wings (see Figure 3.5). It travels and grows.

In 2009, when we realized Nagpur, Maharashtra (our headquarters city) was the gateway to the world's top tiger-sighting destination (Kanha, Madya Pradesh), we began calling it "The Tiger Capital of the World" in newspaper interviews and videos.

Now, Nagpur is being branded as "Tiger Capital of India" for the G20 Meeting, to be held later this year, headed by the Indian Prime Minister (Choudhari, 2023).

We couldn't be more pleased.

An organization and a city now have brands with wings.

Chapter 4
People

The People We Serve

The people of Kanha we work with face 60–70% unemployment. When they can find jobs, they generally receive about USD 2 a day. They sow and reap one crop a year – rice – during rainy season.

As part of the community, we wanted to help. As neighbors who have something to give – assistance, connections for economic growth, education and microfinance to help people help themselves, etc. – we want to help and to see our community grow.

We started by spending time with our neighbors, watching, listening, and asking about their lives and needs – not flinging solutions at them, envisioned from our own perspective.

This approach is inherent in design thinking (DT, one of my favorite fields to work in) and has created huge business value across the globe by ensuring that we first understand what people need and want, and only *then* design breakthrough solutions for them.

In fact, one of my favorite DT stories is of an international development organization that funded a multimillion-dollar water system for a set of rural villages. They thought they would receive a multitude of thanks from the women and children who'd spent countless hours carrying water in jugs on their heads. Instead, the flabbergasted women asked a question.

"How could you do this to us?"

Well-intentioned though they were, the executives who oversaw the project had never talked to the intended users to understand how it would affect their lives.

Going out to fetch water was the only chance for a woman in a traditional home and village to go out, see her friends, and talk. Not only did they support each other emotionally and socially, but this was how information was shared on how to treat children's illnesses, who might be a good marriage match for one's son, subsistence-farming equipment that could be lent from one family to another, etc.

https://doi.org/10.1515/9783110783179-004

The executives had basically shut down the women's face-to-face internet.

When they listened more, the executives found that the women wanted something very simple – an item that would prevent illnesses that damaged everyone's health and kept children out of school, women out of their vegetable gardens, and men out of their agricultural fields – water filters. In fact, if the filters could be made locally, that would provide income and ensure affordability.

The executives provided the water filters and training. I've never heard of them providing a maintenance budget for the unwanted water system.

Thankfully, we didn't make that mistake.

We met informally and formally with community members, individually and together. I think we were the first people who actually *asked* them what they wanted – even showing them laptop images of what might be possible.

I don't think anyone had ever shown them a laptop in 2004. Keep in mind that only 1 in 10 people in India had a mobile phone back then – and they were concentrated in more wealthy segments of the population than ours.

So what did our neighbors tell us?

They told us they need healthcare and education. The nearest clinic was 60 km away (37 miles), and although there was a school building, there was often no teacher and generally no materials. Children were effectively unable to begin their formal education until age 10.

So, we focused on healthcare and education and took action elsewhere we could with whatever we had.

> There's far too much talk and too much time spent on plans. Just do it. Get going with whatever you have, and when people see your good work, resources will come. — Sister Cyril Mooney, Nun, Loreto School Principal, and Kolkata Mary Ward Social Centre programs founder that transformed 450,000 lives

We believed it would grow, and indeed, it has – just not in the ways we initially foresaw (that never happens!). We started with ad-hoc medical camps and had visions of regular camps (which we're doing now, with sponsorship from CMS Info Systems Ltd.), then a local clinic/hospital in future.

We partnered with Sister Cyril Mooney, an education innovator and school principal who was awarded the Padma Shri by the Indian government and represented the nation internationally at educational conferences. Unfortunately, we were stymied with the need for a school building in this place that fluctuates every year between −2 °C (28°F) and 43°C (109°F). We also have monsoon rains from mid-June to September. Sister Cyril provided specifications for building and supplies, and she appointed a teacher who came and advised us for a future time when we could start a primary school. We didn't partner with government for the use of the existing school building, given substantial complications that would be inherent in such a project between government and a private organization, in which one was already established, and one was not.

In the meantime, we pursued vocational education for women (a much smaller group who could fit into a rented building), and opportunities came along to do good in ways we hadn't envisioned before.

So we took them.

They – and programs we added to our portfolio later – are described more fully below. People associate all of these initiatives with us. Some of them reduce human-animal conflict and reliance on the tiger's habitat for survival.

Medical Camps

At these events, which were advertised by word-of-mouth, and coordinated by phone and WhatsApp, we've treated 4,100 patients so far. Early on, CARE Hospital in Nagpur provided doctors, medicines, and treatment. More recently, we've run them with our new healthcare partner, Tilda Medical Hospital (only 180 km from Kanha instead of 250; easier and cheaper for families to travel to and stay near). Now that we have a corporate sponsor (CMS Info Systems Ltd.), we plan to host a camp each quarter, which may raise patient visits to 2,400 per year.

For the most recent camp, the government agreed to donate the use of an as yet unstaffed hospital so our medical partner could deliver services alongside the TTC team in a medical facility. Over the years, we've treated a range of conditions including bacterial infections, jaundice, malaria, pregnancy-related issues, tuberculosis, viral fevers, and much more. In more serious cases, patients are offered hospitalization with our medical partner. Over the years, this has included removing a 5 kg tumor from a patient's abdomen and subsidizing a life-saving kidney operation for a woman with a 2-year-old child. She is now alive, well, and raising her son.

We may introduce Vaxess Technologies as a vaccine supplier, since they provide shelf-stable vaccines that eliminate refrigeration mistakes (which render vaccines ineffective) and 80% of the inoculation industry's cost – refrigeration.

For vaccines they do not supply, and when we have a more continuous medical presence (not just once a quarter), with permanent quarters with appropriate security, we envision adding a solar-powered refrigerator. This would not only house vaccines but also snake antivenom. We live among cobras and other serpentine species which – with the right antivenom administered appropriately – need not issue a death sentence with every bite.

Snake Catch and Release

Cobras and other serpents regularly establish homes in or near where humans have established homes. They seek dark, damp, cool places (like bathrooms or root cellars) and search for small animals for food (e.g., rats and mice, which are attracted to human food).

In monsoon season, all forest animals seek shelter, and power supply is often disrupted. Without lights, it's easy to disturb a snake and receive a bite in return.

Armed with bravery, keen naturalist skills, a solar light (donated by Krishna Daga), and special tools like a catch-and-hold snake bag, our resident artist, Ashish Kachwaha, captures and releases serpents back into the wild, maintaining the safety of both humans and wildlife.

As part of our medical and snake interventions, we'll pursue acquiring and/or developing shelf-stable antivenom with Vaxess, which could be the second global life-saving breakthrough for emerging economies, after vaccines.

How so?

Snakebite affects 4.5 million people each year, globally, causing serious injury to 2.7 million, and death to 125,000 (Global Snakebite Initiative, n.d.).

Which country hosts the most snakebite deaths?

India.

According to a study by the Indian Council of Medical Research (Dayanidhi, 2022), half of all snakebite cases in the world originate in India, resulting in nearly 47,000 deaths each year.

Sadly, only 30% of snakebite victims in rural India are treated in-hospital.

Snakebite has been called "the most neglected tropical disease."

Perhaps we should change that.

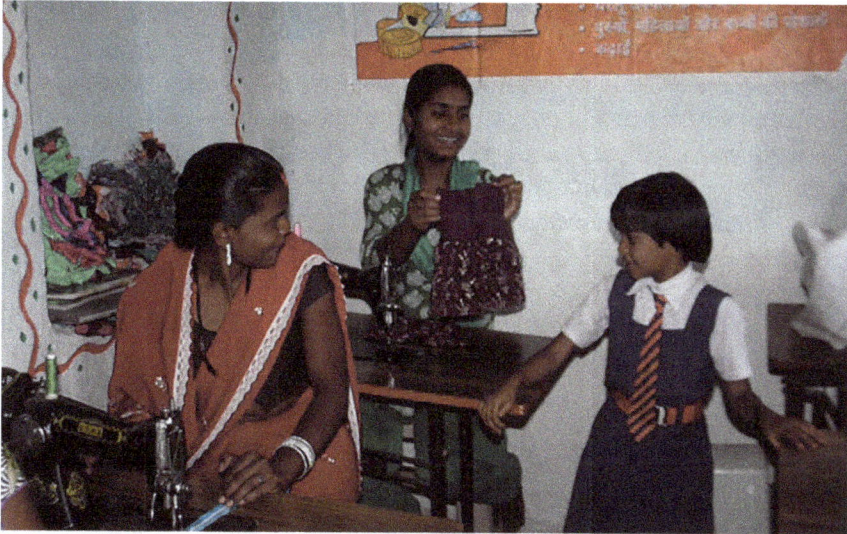

Figure 4.1: Sewing students and a happy customer.

Usha Sewing Schools

In partnership with Usha International, we established two Usha Tiger Center Silai Sewing Schools, in which women gain skills and certification in sewing (see Figure 4.1). The curriculum was designed by the National Institute of Fashion Design (NIFD), based in New Delhi.

Pre-COVID, those two schools could train 60 students in our 6-month program, held twice a year, plus advanced workshops to upgrade their skills. Now, we're combining them into one school and are re-opening. In fact, it might be possible to expand it into a training-and-production center in the future.

Once students graduate with a diploma, they can apply for a microloan from a bank that formally recognizes the qualification. Upon approval, the graduate can launch a tailoring business. Over 150 women have done so, and we couldn't be prouder of the hard work, learning, and achievement they've accomplished.

Now over 150 women (families, actually) can earn a living.

The schools also serve our environmental mission, since they're 100% solar-powered and equipped with water filters to keep teachers and students healthy and studying. Now, Usha is encouraging its other 26,000+ schools in nearly 16,000 villages across India to do so as well (NDTV, 2022).

Forest Waste Furniture Factory

Nishi was passing by some forest workers one day and noticed them removing, piling, and burning lantana. He learned that it's actually an invasive species that overwhelms native flora and is regularly cut back. Since the material resembles rattan, a forest vine used to make wicker furniture and baskets, he wondered if lantana could be used the same way.

Indeed it can.

Even better, the Forest Service is happy to donate it to us.

We established a factory – a comfortable, useful workspace for up to 50 men – that enables farmers to earn money off-season turning forest waste (lantana) into useful, sellable products.

They've done well, and we applaud their creations.

We also learned something about the men and women in our community. When asked if men should be included in the Usha Sewing Schools and women should also work in the factory, the community said no.

Men and women both have opportunities, and they enjoy their own workspaces just fine. There's no need to reengineer a society they're quite happy with. Just help them generate opportunities and grow in ways they see fit.

So that's what we'll do – instructions noted.

Beekeeping

When people enter the forest seeking honey (or firewood, cattle fodder, medicinal plants, and other essentials), they risk startling a tiger. The big cats can be resting anywhere (especially in tall grass) and don't like to be startled. When seeking honey, there's also the risk of bees fighting back.

So, in collaboration with the Centre of Science for Villages (CSV) – courtesy of our own MD, Prof. Nishi Mukerji, who is also Vice Chairman of CSV – an entire village of Baigas from Amantola Village, as well as some men from Khatiya Village, travelled to Wardha (CSV headquarters) to learn beekeeping.

Because housing is provided (not self-made), the bees make more honey than they need. The excess can be used by beekeepers or, if they too have excess, can be processed and sold in the marketplace. This increases both safety in our community and entrepreneurial income.

It has created quite the buzz in the market.

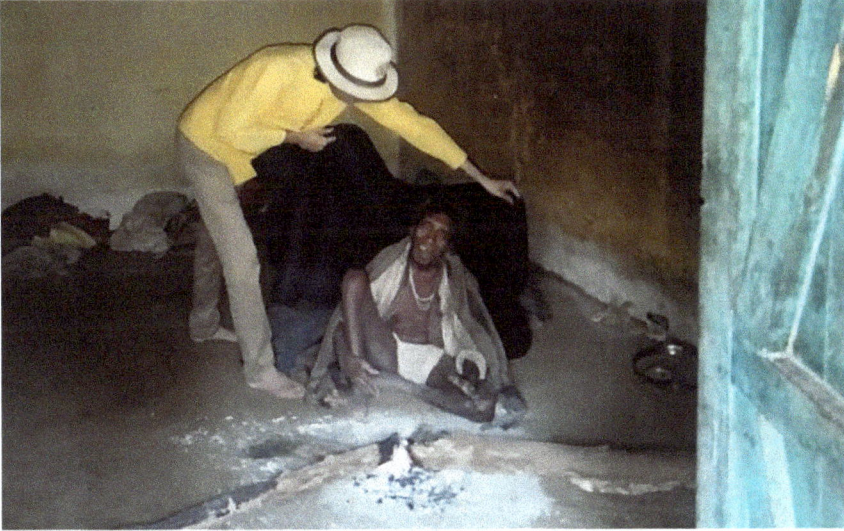

Figure 4.2: Ashish Kachwaha giving a blanket to a community member.

Essentials Giving

We've given blankets, clothing, household goods, and water filters to nearly 25,000 people over the years (see Figure 4.2).

Not only do blankets and clothing provide needed warmth, but they may reduce the need for firewood gathered from the forest (which can precede a tiger or snake encounter).

In cities, new clothing for children can also ward off child snatchers who would sell humans. (Children who appear neglected are more targeted.) Although we're not in a city, at very minimum, it gives our children a boost and reinforces that someone cares about them and that they are worthy of good.

Water filters are a key gift to our community, as well. Nearly 38 million people a year in India are affected by diseases caught from unclean water. (We suspect it's many more, since reported figures can only be estimated from clinic and hospital visits.)

In fact, 80% of diseases are water-borne. Over 1.5 million children die from diarrhea, and the economy loses USD 600 million each year, as a result of 73 million absences due to illness (Khambete, 2019).

Giving water filters to homes and using water filters at our sewing schools and furniture factory prevent illness, improve wellbeing, and make people more productive. It also lightens the load on our medical camps so doctors can focus on other illnesses.

After all, to make the most of what we have and what we do, we focus on strategies and actions that synergize and reinforce each other.

Fusion works.

Figure 4.3: Baiga dance and a Baiga hug for Nishi.

Baiga Cultural Programs and COVID Campaign

Song and dance are essential elements of the Baiga tribal customs and traditions (see Figure 4.3). When we realized the beauty and cultural significance of Baiga tribal dance, we helped arrange events to share their artistic achievements and rich culture with tourists and the broader community.

Not only do their performances raise awareness of their culture locally, nationally, and internationally (via tourists), but these events provide them with essential earnings.

The nature reserve authorities learned of these events and now host dances every day at the Khatiya forest entry gate. Recognizing the potential of such activities for economic growth through travel, the Chief Minister of Maharashtra appointed Nishi to the State Ecotourism Board, where he can further influence public policy for growth and good.

Now, the tribes earn money every day, and visitors learn more about the tribal people of our area. Harmony grows among the indigenous community, non-tribal neighbors, government, and the broader community of man.

Once COVID struck, tourism and public gatherings were restricted, which of course hampered the Baigas' dance earnings. However, now (post-pandemic) they've resumed operations and are invited to dance at public and private celebrations, e.g., official welcomes and special occasions, both at the forest gate and all over our region

To make matters worse, rumors spread in our area that COVID injections were of no use, so people refrained from taking the vaccines. To combat unfounded rumors and promote health and safety in our community, tribal leader Sonsay Baiga publicly took his shot. Thousands of people saw his injection-taking image smiling at them on social media, word spread, and the Baiga community followed his lead, taking their injections, too.

To help further promote COVID vaccines, Baiga tribal artists composed and performed songs in non-restricted areas about taking the vaccines. They promoted the vaccines and everyone's health and safety across all our local villages, saving who knows how many lives.

They travel long distances to deliver such messages and share their art and culture. After our most recent medical camp, for example, they came from up to 100 km away (over 60 miles) to dance in celebration of that camp's 600 patient-visits successfully delivered.

No matter how developed we become, we pray we'll always take time to follow their wise practice and celebrate good.

Figure 4.4: The Kanha Sarai Art Gallery.

Artwork and Art Gallery

At the request of the local government, our resident artist, Ashish Kachwaha, gathered a team and began painting Mandla's town wall with art depicting the Baiga's environmentally-friendly lifestyle and culture. A community project, the mural not only promotes eco-friendliness and indigenous culture, but harmony among the community members who contribute.

In addition, Ashish (mainly a painter and drawer) launched the Kanha Sarai Art Gallery (see Figure 4.4) near the Khatiya gate of the reserve. In it, his and sculptor Manoj Trivedi's profound drawings, paintings, and sculptures promote art and culture (1) *of* local artists and (2) *about* local wildlife and people – the Baiga tribals, who traditionally serve as guardians of the forest, living a life that takes no more from nature than they need. Ashish's works have been exhibited in New Delhi (at the famous Tribeni Art Gallery), Kolkata (at the renowned Tollygunge Club), and listed with an international art dealer in France. His and Manoj's creations are also proudly displayed in Singapore on a permanent basis.

Chief Justice of India, Sharad Bobde, and Governor of Chattisgarh, Anu Suya Bai, both visited the gallery and received some of the inspiring artwork, which will further spread their messages to other illustrious viewers who can make an impact through their policies and professions.

Art and Eco-Education Partnership

Inspired by the above, we've partnered with Ashish, create2donate, and the Albatross Foundation to sell select pieces of his artwork to further the mission of all three. Albatross (albatrossglobal.org) provides free education promoting sustainable development and has trained more than 13,000 children in China, Brazil, and France on sustainability and why it's important. It has distributed more than 45,000 Albatross-developed "green education" books and provides mobile apps as well (scientific and multilingual). Ashish's paintings are hosted in an art gallery in Lyon, France, pending sale per the create2donate (c2d) business model – 1/3 of proceeds remitted each to the artist, c2d, and Albatross, to further all their good works.

> Photography is the only "language" understood in allparts of the world, and bridging all nations andcultures, it links the family of man . . . it reflectstruthfully life and events, allows us to share in the hopes and despair of others, and illuminates politicaland social conditions. We become the eyewitnesses of the humanity and inhumanity of mankind. — Helmut Gernsheim

Photography

To raise funds and raise awareness (and just because we love photography!), we crafted three coffee table books and a digital collection, with ITC's design collaboration and generous printing donation. Further, they donated the use of the back covers of their blank schoolbooks, sold to schoolchildren across the nation. We placed a photo of our spokestiger, a brief message, and our website address.

They sold 2.5 million copies.

We owe them both thanks and congratulations for raising awareness in the next generation who will care for the planet and its resources.

Figure 4.5: The Rajurkar's only photograph of their deceased son, Ram.

The Most Important Photo We Ever Took

Nishi called me one day with the sad news that a member of our community had died – a young man named Ram Rajurkar (see Figure 4.5). I was sad to hear of this great loss but also surprised that he told me I'd photographed him.

Nishi said it was a photo from years before at nearby Birwa Airport, when a private plane landed, carrying executives for a meeting about the upcoming resort. He was one of the people in front of the plane.

Since I'm neurotically organized and digital-friendly, I found it fairly quickly in the files on my hard drive and shared several candidates with him.

He identified the one.

Nishi then took the digital image to a printing store and had a print made and framed. He presented it to the young man's parents, Chetram and Basanti Rajurkar, with our condolences.

They were overwhelmed.

They hung it in a place of honor in their home and now can see their son every day. They told Nishi (and he shared with me) something we hadn't imagined.

It was the only photo of their son they ever had.

Living in a world where 1.81 trillion photos are captured every year – 5 billion a day – 57,246 every second – we were shocked (Broz, 2023).

Clearly, it was the most important photo we ever took. We realized photography can have a bigger impact than just enjoying pretty pictures – whether to grieving parents (deep impact) or 2.5 million schoolchildren receiving a message of sustainability (broad impact).

In sum, our programs do two things:

–   provide benefits people associate with the tiger, via our name and our conservation message

–   reduce human-animal conflict, via interim funding for tiger-harmed farm animals, snake capture and release, and beekeeping (which reduces the need to go into the forest, sometimes startling a tiger).

Figure 4.6: The Tiger Center Team.

The People Who Serve

> I don't know what your destiny will be, but one thing
> I do know: the only ones among you who will be
> really happy are those who have sought and found
> how to serve.
> — Albert Schweitzer

The TTC team (see Figure 4.6) "comes from" France, India, Ireland, Italy, Malaysia, Philippines, Singapore, Vietnam, UK, and USA, when we take account of place of birth as well as citizenship. In fact, many of us as individuals have multiple nationalities we could claim, based on birth, citizenship, and/or residence.

Most of us also have a rich array of professions (again, some individuals having multiple), from junior through very senior people. They study, work, or are retired from art, academics, architecture, business/industry, culinary arts, eco-consulting, education, entrepreneurship, faith, farming, government service, hospitality, information technology, law, law enforcement, marketing, medicine, naturalist services, not-for-profit, psychology, tribal or village leadership, and tourism.

They bring their heads, hearts, and hands to work whether in person "on the ground" or remote, via technology.

They are also generous with their time, as busy people staffing an organization and running projects on a completely voluntary basis, so far.

Basically, we are a synergy (or fusion), integrating:

- **Nations and Fields** – as above
- **Multiple Faiths** – Meetings and special events (e.g., tree-planting on the land) begin with interfaith prayer, and our mission is rooted in faith-based giving and stewardship.
- **Family and Business** – We manage TTC using business principals, but it grew from and remains rooted in our "Fusion Family" of different colors, genders, and ages, from different nations, with different citizenships and languages (see Meadows, 2015 TEDx talk, available on this book's webpage, drcjmeadows.com/ sustainability). Our affection and care extend to friends and community, as well, whom we hold dear. In fact, in the same way family stories never die (meaning you'll be teased for a variety of funny blunders for the rest of your life), community stories become folklore that never dies. I continually (and happily) hear about the time I went to a wedding in the community and got my sari stuck in the stand fan. It's now a running but endearing joke.
- **"High-Tech" and "Low-Tech"** – Our activities range from hands-on medical care and essentials giving to internet and smartphone communication with the team and our extended supporters and followers via social media.
- **Men and Women** – In a nation like India, rooted in gender traditions, it is refreshing – and important – to see men and women working together seamlessly on an equal basis. With both male and female community leaders and a woman chairman, we hope to serve as an example for the next generation.
- **Multi-Generational Work** – Increasingly, companies will need to facilitate collaboration in a workforce that ranges from Gen Z (and beyond) through senior citizens. We already do that and find multi-generational perspectives a key element of our creative diversity.

- **"Walks of Life"** – From Baiga tribal to Gond agriculturalist to retired corporate executive to international technology leaders (and more), our team spans diverse socio-economic positions and collaborates as colleagues.
- **The Four Ages of Man** – In discussing our amazing team with Nishi, I realized that since the Baigas are manly a hunting and gathering people, the Gonds are agricultural, the villagers use machinery (e.g., the occasional tractor) indicative of the industrial age, and some of us earn a living as knowledge- and creative-workers with technology, we actually span the four ages of man. It is a remarkable feeling to know that history is alive and well in us in our current moment in time and that we can all work together. There is something essentially human in that.

We thank our world-class advisory board for stellar advice on policy, business, legal, eco, and human trends and technologies that help us all grow. We are grateful every day for our stellar on-the-ground leaders and achievers. As a family-based community organization, we are excited about our family's next generation of leaders and are proud of the interests and skills they can contribute to our community. We salute our founding members who have passed away but remain with us "in memoriam." Not only have they helped shape our organization and the vision we uphold, but we will hold their friendship in our hearts forever. They live on in their families, the community, and with us in The Tiger Center. We carry the memory of them with us and seek to continue the work they loved and achieved so well. May we honor them in all that we do and all we continue to uphold, as they would have wished.

We recognize each of these individuals, listed in Table 4.1.

Table 4.1: The Tiger Center Team.

Part of the Organization	Name	Title
Board of Directors	Dr. CJ Meadows	Executive Chairman
	Prof. Nishikant Mukerji	Managing Director
	Advocate Sudhir Puranik	Board Director
Advisory Board (Non-Executive)	Chaitanya Jagdale Dr. Chris Marshall	Advisory Board Director Visionary Co-Founder and Advisory Board Director
	Dr. Ghislaine Bouillet-Cordonnier, Esq.	Legal Consultant and Advisory Board Director
	Dr. Kristina Taioli	Advisory Board Director
	Awantika Chitnavis	Consulting Architect and Advisory Board Director
	Patrick C. Willis	Advisory Board Director
	Sister Cyril Mooney	Education Consultant and Advisory Board Director
	N. Srinivasan	Eco-development Advisor and Advisory Board Director
Leaders and Achievers	Commissioner R. Mehta	Head Of Community Programs
	Ashish Kachwaha	Artist and Naturalist
	Rano Lakhera	Project Manager
	Sonsay Baiga	Baiga Ambassador and Tribal Leader
	Babeeta Lakhera	Vocational School Principal
	Kura Bai Chhapri	Gond Ambassador and Women's Community Leader
	Salim	Naturalist and Driver
	Mallu Singh	Naturalist and Guide
Next-Gen	Jonathan Marshall	Lay Minister for Christian Youth
	Anna Marshall	Quatra Linguist and Volunteer English Teacher
	David Marshall	Wildlife Seeker and Videographer
	Sarah Marshall	Animal Rights Advocate and Volunteer Teacher

Table 4.1 (continued)

Part of the Organization	Name	Title
In Memoriam	Anand Jagdale	Visionary Co-Founder and Executive Director
	Manglu Baiga	Legendary Co-Founder of the Kanha Nature Reserve
	Phiroz Patel	Tiger Center Founding Team Member
	Sami Mohammad	Sarpanch (Village Head) and Advocate
	Sidhi Singh	Former Sarpanch (Village Head) and Advocate
	Nanhey Singh	Advisor and Ex-Principal Home Secretary and Member of The Human Rights Commission for the Government of Madhya Pradesh

Chapter 5
Conclusions, Insights, and Ways Forward

> We're just getting started. We're just beginning to
> meet what will be the future – we've got the
> Model T.
> — Grace Murray Hopper, US Navy and
> computer industry icon who pioneered machine-
> independent programming languages and led her
> team to develop the first computer compiler (COBOL)

In this book, we've explored:
- facts, figures, and synergies between people, profit, and planet particular to The Tiger Center but generalizable, as well, to other species, other environments, other people, and other organizations that integrate triple-bottom-line mission, goals, and measures of success
- the journey of one organization working at the intersection of all three, with insights and implications to consider and enact in your own situation (see insights section below)
- broader understanding of the different facets and levels of "sustainability"
    - planet – which must be both protected as a natural asset and made productive in positive ways, encouraging further protection. Green accounting, legislation, and wise analysis of environmental impact (which can lead to profitable business improvements) can help
    - profit – which should be generated with a business model that will weather economic ups and downs, instead of flourishing in good times, only to be cut off when times are hard. Social enterprise structure and triple-bottom-line management can help. ESG can also help organizations operate more sustainably, in both the environmental sense and the business sense. It makes good sense
    - people – who need to survive and thrive economically, and who need to associate that support with the environment that only they can protect on a mass scale. Further, organizations can design their products, services, and systems to remove human-animal and human-environmental conflict
    - person – who may be a chairman or a farmer, producer or consumer. We are uplifted by serving a mission we value, but we also need others' help. Don't do it alone. We accomplish more together and can support each other emotionally (and in many other ways) along the way. Don't

https://doi.org/10.1515/9783110783179-005

over-push and over-stress when things aren't working and you might try another way, or when now's not the time. Each of us as individuals needs to survive and thrive, as well

All of us at TTC pray that our work furthers our mission. Perhaps even bigger is our prayer that it also inspires others to help people, profit, and planet in their own way.

Results . . . So Far

We're thrilled to have just received the award for Social Enterprise Innovator of the Year 2023 India from Acquisition International, based in the UK. It's a well-earned pat on the back for our very hard-working team. Even more exciting is the impact we've made so far – and more to come.

Tigers: Increase

Our forest has experienced a 4X increase in tiger numbers since we began operations in 2004 (Forest Department of Madhya Pradesh, personal communication, 2023). We can't take credit for all of that growth, since the Forest Department and many others had an impact. What we can say is that we've encouraged us all to work together and are thrilled to see people, planet, and profit (the local economy) growing together.

In fact, the tiger population growth has caused a new problem: fighting for territory. To reduce tiger losses from other tigers, new "retirement" sections of the forest have been set aside for the older tigers who become targets for younger males seeking to establish territory.

Do we see the increase in tiger population only in the forest? No.

During the COVID pandemic, when streets were quiet and largely free from traffic, tigers began street walking (so to speak) and loitering in the villages.

Can we relax our vigilance? No.

Approximately 20–25 tigers are poached every year – a never-ending threat (Banerjee, 2015).

Was Sariska the last tragedy to wipe out an entire local tiger population? No.

Five years later, the same thing happened in the Panna Tiger Reserve (Banerjee, 2015).

However, with five re-introduced tigers (from within the state – Rajasthan), improved security, reconnaissance satellites, and village relocation, Sariska held 20 tigers in 2020 – and growing (Wikipedia, Sariska Tiger Reserve).

In Panna, six tigers were relocated (again, from within the state – Madya Pradesh), after which 32 cubs were born (26 survived), and poaching was stopped.

Despite the successes, the fact that one relocated tiger in Sariska died from poisoning would suggest that the local people still need to be added into the conservation plans.

Environment: Public Policy, Eco-Technologies, and Awareness

In some places, local people are included in conservation policy and programs. For example, in certain buffer-area villages (i.e., those around an unpopulated core) local people have been inducted into forest patrol taskforces. The Special Tiger Protection Force (STPF) was established in 2008 under the National Tiger Conservation Authority and works to eliminate poaching.

On the other side of the equation – demand for tiger parts (e.g., for Chinese medicine) – efforts are also underway between tiger-conservation leaders in countries like India, China, Nepal, and the Russian Federation (among others) to reduce the tiger trade and regulate tiger farming (done mainly in China).

Movement of public human roadways out of the reserves and provision of wildlife corridors – so animals can travel from one habitat and its population to another – are also important for discouraging poaching and for helping tigers thrive and repopulate with gene diversity.

We've also seen some surprises. Siberian and Sumatran tiger populations are growing, and the clouded leopard – declared extinct in 2013 – was sighted in a remote area of Taiwan. Korea's De-Militarized Zone (DMZ) has become an inadvertent refuge for rare birds and other species – apparently including tigers, after 20 years of tracking and research. Other nations, such as Vietnam and Laos might also benefit from human- and economy-inclusive conservation policies and tracking research in their most remote areas.

In our own location, and after many discussions with government officials about Kanha's amazing potential for night safaris and a 12-month business season, they changed their policies so part of the park (at the Kanha-Kisli gate, near us) is open year-round. They also approved night safaris (see Figure 5.1). That's good news for tourists and for the community that supports them.

Having promoted and used eco-friendly technologies for many years, we're proud not only to have helped our local population begin using solar devices and water filters, but to have influenced Usha Silai Sewing Schools to promote the use of solar power for their 26,000+ affiliated schools in nearly 16,000 villages across India.

Figure 5.1: Wild tiger during one of our night safaris.

Finally, we are thankful to R. Srinivasan at our printing sponsor, ITC Ltd., not only for printing our fund-raising books, but also for helping us reach 2.5 million schoolchildren in India with our message of conservation (on the back of ITC's blank workbooks) – the next generation to protect the tiger, forest, and broader environment.

People: Benefits

Kanha has grown as an ecotourist destination, and employment and income for our community have grown with it. We're not solely responsible, but we do take part in encouraging and popularizing that growth with all the programs described above. Our programs provide a range of benefits, from economic (e.g., tailoring shops and the lantana furniture factory) to social (e.g., medical camps and arts and culture initiatives). Our community is fiercely protective of our tigers and environment, and we pray that continues and grows.

In sum, the TTC impact highlights include:

– 2.5 million schoolchildren have received TTC's conservation message
– 26,000+ schools in nearly 16,000 villages across India are being encouraged by Usha International to do as we've done – run on clean (solar) energy and use water filters
– nearly 25,000 people have received blankets, clothing, household goods, and water filters

- 4,100 patient visits have been provided through medical camps
- 150+ sewing school students have graduated, many launching tailoring businesses
- 50 men can now work in the lantana furniture factory, supporting their families in farming off-season
- A whole tribal community (the Baigas) now earns a regular income sharing their music, dance, and culture
- An entire village of Baigas, plus a group of men from Khatiya Village, are able to supply their own needs and earn an income from beekeeping

Benefits to TTC

We recognize and are thankful for all the community, government, and environment have given us, as well, including:
- guardianship of the tiger and environment we all depend on
- placement of a new water reservoir next to our land, which attracts wildlife people will come to see
- placement of a new forest gate near us
- opening our section of the forest during monsoon, extending the tourist season from 9 to 12 months
- trust and brotherhood (sisterhood, too, of course!) of a great community

We began nearly 20 years ago with a vision to serve, and despite severe setbacks and personal tragedy during the global crisis of 2008, loss of team members, the COVID pandemic, and more, people have trusted that we're true to our word and that we would continue serving.

We have.

We're thankful for the opportunities we've been given to influence public policy, proliferate eco-tech, and save lives and livelihoods in multiple ways described above, but it is important to recognize what underpins it all and serves as the foundation for future progress: trust – from those we advise and those we serve.

We are truly grateful for it.

Figure 5.2: TTC's "footprint" extends well beyond the local village.

Footprint Beyond Kanha

We launched our "Golden Triangle" model of conservation in 2004 and have been thrilled to see similar work done elsewhere – whether via our example or merely by great minds thinking alike (as the saying goes) (see Figure 5.2). We applaud them.

In Melghat Tiger Reserve, for example, the administration has been promoting villagers' livelihood in the core and buffer zones via computer and self-employment trade education (including sewing machine tailoring for local women), as well as providing 4-wheel vehicles (and purchase subsidies) to tribal families – and helping them obtain driving licenses (some for heavy vehicles).

In the Peyriar Tiger Reserve (in Kerala), programs are people-oriented and encourage ecotourism. Their Eco-Development Committees (EDCs), launched in 2005–2006, are staffed by local communities (Dasgupta, 2015). They implemented the India Eco-Development Project (IEDP), which aims to conserve bio-diversity with local participation and won the UN-India Biodiversity Governance award for holistic management. They achieved "Field Learning Centre" status from the Ministry of Environment and Forests for their successful efforts (Dasgupta, 2015). Their human-inclusive approach to conservation, has resulted in new schools for communities, growth of ecotourist businesses and jobs, and a positive impact on the environment on which people depend.

As illustrated with these examples, the Golden Triangle model of conservation – including species, environment, and people – is applicable to other places. Other species should benefit from the approach as well.

Integrating policy and action for both the environment and the economy is also applicable everywhere and scalable worldwide.

It just takes (but is harder than it looks!) integrating the people who make government policies, business decisions, and social programs at global, national, regional, and local levels. Publicizing new ideas like the Golden Triangle and case examples like those above are also needed, to help us move forward in this way.

In fact, maybe we're working in a new (integrated) field – eco-eco-development, human-centered conservation, or holistic growth. Whatever the case, we'll need stakeholders from a variety of fields addressing all parts of the challenge to collaborate and co-create new strategies, structures, and systems, if we're going to make a difference.

In short, it takes a village to save a tiger (and its forest) – and to save ourselves.

Insights

We learned some valuable lessons in our journey, outlined below. We hope you can put them to use in yours.

Your Biggest Opportunities are God-Given

This all started with buying unusual land in unusual circumstances, priced (miraculously?) the same as a wage settlement after an ethical act (warning of an impending crisis).

You have to be open to opportunities when they're given to you (if you want to take the really big ones, that is). You don't generate them yourself. And you don't build them alone. The best opportunities come to you, come to life, and grow with their own spirit and energy.

Further, if you can be trusted with little, you can usually be trusted with much. The crisis Nishi warned corporate leaders about cost millions. Perhaps the opportunity we received – once we all create more good with it – will yield even more, not just to ourselves, but to the economy (community included) and the environment (tiger included), in our location and beyond.

Someday, perhaps we'll analyze the impact. For now, we'll focus on making an impact.

Economy and Environment: The Numbers are Shocking

The studies in the Planet chapter – and many more not shared here – tell a surprising story of the economic value and impact of our natural assets. When a shark or a tiger bring USD 200,000 and more to the economy, or when a heritage tree provides USD 120,000 of services, why would you kill one for a few hundred or even a few thousand dollars?

Simple: the people who take the quick-and-easy economic gain are not concerned with other stakeholders, and the other stakeholders – people who have their environment and economy at stake – don't know they're in danger. They probably don't know they could act as guardians instead of bystanders and don't know what to do about it.

Organized efforts to include them would help, such as induction into the Special Tiger Protection Force (STPF) or even programs in the neighborhood watch style in places officials can't patrol enough. Technology can also help – for example, satellite-based tiger tracking, e-eye surveillance for early poaching alerts, drones, and MSTrIPES and camera-tap systems already in use in tiger reserves. For trees, a South American rainforest initiative straps mobile phones to trees for surveillance and tracking of illegal logging.

We need not only security for our assets but also to employ them wisely and to ensure those benefits go to everyone, so everyone has a clear stake in the economically-powered environment.

People Must Be Part of Conservation Plans

This is clear, not only from the Sariska and Panna tragedies described above but also from the growth in wellbeing of the tigers, environments, and communities where people are included in ecological policies and programs.

Start by Listening to Needs, Not Flinging Solutions

Development organizations have made the mistake – repeatedly – of using only top-down analysis to guide their program decisions. As we see in the water system example above, the top-down approach should be integrated with bottom-up, as with design thinking (DT) projects.

Instead of starting with solutions, we need to think like designers, first understanding challenges, needs, and desires of the people for whom we design. In other words, don't solve a problem before you understand it. Obvious, but all too common. The design thinking process begins by spending time with people – watching, listening, asking about their lives, challenges, needs, and desires.

It's important also to understand that designers don't just gather specifications and take orders for what to deliver. Users are not designers. They may not know how anyone else's life is different or what might be possible with technology. Designers put themselves in the circumstance of their users and design what would make life better – what the designer would want in their place.

Never Let Your Husband and Brother Wine-Talk While You're Diapering Babies Late at Night

If you do, then don't agree to lead and build whatever they come up with – unless you're ready for a radical opportunity and entrepreneurial roller-coaster ride of a lifetime.

Entrepreneurs Envision, But Others May Think It's a Promise

When we first began to ask people about their lives, challenges, needs, and desires, we shared our thoughts on possible solutions.

Beware.

If you're an entrepreneur, you think in terms of possibilities and may naturally share them. Listeners, however, if they're more accustomed to hearing new government or corporate initiatives that have already been approved and budgeted, may not hear you say, "We might."

They're accustomed to hearing promises, not possibilities.

When we discussed possible initiatives with our community and then couldn't make them real in the wake of the global economic crisis of 2008, it was a disappointment to them (understandably) and hard to understand. It shook their trust in us. We worked hard to regain that trust and are very careful, now, to communicate in ways that do not raise false hopes – but instead raise hope where it's warranted.

Create a Whole-Brained Team and Appreciate Your Creative Dissonance

I've already advised, "Don't do initiatives like TTC on your own – get a team." But some teams are better than others. Teams that include diverse skills, knowledge, fields, and both thinking and action styles are the best. You'll need all of them to co-create better together than as individuals. You'll also need co-creation skills for ideation and more, which you can learn – for example, from design thinking. Additional diversity such as gender, nationality, and more also help.

Co-creation isn't a buzzword for never-ending agreement, however. You'll need creative dissonance (honesty, questioning, and more). To make your dissonance creative instead of destructive, invest in understanding your team as individuals (psychometrics help here) and sharing the value that each should recognize in each other.

Network, Not Hierarchy

Top-down, hierarchical organizations can be very effective for delivery, but they're generally not as good at change and innovation as a network in which everyone questions, gathers information, and contributes more equally. In fact, networked organizations need not own the whole production process. They partner and operate in an ecosystem of current and potential partners, suppliers, distributors, and other stakeholders who are not only useful for program delivery but are also useful for innovation – new ideas, contacts, and more.

We didn't need to do everything, own everything, and control everything. The mission and vision tied our stakeholders together, and relationships and win-wins were managed.

In fact, it was the team – not a hierarchy – that kept TTC going during hard times. For that, I am very grateful.

The Most Important Capital: Creative, Social, and Trust

Business – alongside other forms of organization – runs on trust. If you trust in a fair marketplace, then you can buy from anyone. If not, then you'll need to trust in the particular parties you deal with. If you don't know them, you might trust in a brand name and deal with the local representative.

We're able to avoid wasting time and resources verifying our credentials and convincing people of our programs and intentions because the individuals on our team – and now the organization – have earned trust. Our mission, vision, and values clarify for everyone what we're doing with that trust.

Not only do we operate more easily as part of a trusted network of government officials, concerned businesses, and community leaders, but that social network is also valuable capital. When we have problems or want to start something new, we know immediately whom to reach out to for ideas, connections, and help.

That social network includes people who can create and co-create in a variety of ways, which is essential to us as we grow. We don't grow by replicating what we do (although we might consider doing that in future). We grow by expanding what we do and whom we serve.

So, in contrast to an industrial-age organization that relies on financial capital, or a knowledge-age organization that relies on information, we're a creative organization, relying on creative, social, and trust capital. We don't particularly need an economic valuation of that capital but do need to keep it front-of-mind so we can protect and grow it.

Engagement is More Powerful Than Rules

According to Gallup (Pendell, 2022), the world loses USD 7.8 trillion a year in productivity because 80% of our global workforce is either not engaged in their workplace or actively disengaged. The organizations they work for apparently operate on rules and systems, not people.

Are rules better than people at operations?

Not necessarily.

"Work to rule," for example, is a way for workers to go on strike without formally declaring one. Workers follow every rule recorded in the organization's policies and procedures manuals and – of course – get little or nothing done. Rules impede their progress at every turn.

We've found that engagement, based on our mission, vision, and values, is far more effective at aligning behavior and performance than any rules we're accustomed to in larger organizational settings.

We will need to craft more policies, rules, and procedures as we grow, but we're comfortable relying on people for now, since we've observed the same in boutique hospitality companies, boutique consulting firms, and even larger organizations that have shut down some of their rules.

For example, when some companies have removed "sick day" limits, they've seen a reduction in sick days taken. Some have removed declared office hours and instead focus on worker outcomes – which remain the same or increase. Some have thousands of employees, hundreds of millions of dollars of revenues, and make complicated things like rocket fuel systems and not only remove rules but rethink their fundamentals, giving people the right to set and enforce their own rules – with excellent results (Semler, 2014).

So, if you're a small, innovative organization, don't tie yourself down with rules unnecessarily or too soon. If you're a larger one, consider whether you could try de-ruling, too.

Do What You Can Now and Let It Grow

Sister Cyril was right. If we'd waited until we had big corporate sponsors and finalized plans to get started, we never would have. We had to delay the primary school because of weather and other constraints, but we did launch vocational education and all our other programs with whatever resources we could gather.

It'll grow. Others will come and support. But people usually need to see something in operation before they're willing to help you grow it.

Never Pass Up a Chance to Do Good

Again, these are the golden opportunities God hands you – things you wouldn't have thought up on your own. New activities that were not part of our original plan, like art and cultural promotion, beekeeping, and the furniture factory, emerged, the more we spent time in our community. We then crafted ways to help based on deeper insights gained over time with experience. They've worked well and never would have happened unless we'd been open to insight and opportunity.

Never, Never, Never, Never Give In

Churchill was right.

Figure 5.3: Life is better together.

Fusions

> The best solutions come from collaboration between the people with
> the problems to solve and the people who can solve them.
> — Jeff Patton, author

We've seen the power of fusion for ourselves – effectiveness because of integrated diversity (see Figure 5.3). Various elements of fusion are included in the material above. In sum, the following fusions have been either the outcome of our work or the inputs:

- People, profit, and planet
- Ecological-economic development
- Sustainable business theory and practice
- Business, not-for-profit, government, academe, and community
- Family and business
- Multiple faiths
- National origin
- Fields
- "Walks of life"
- The four ages of man
- Men and women
- "Fusioney" people
- "High-tech" and "low-tech"
- Organizational sizes

We'll continue to value our diversity and synergize our outputs.

The Way Forward

About a year before this book was written, Nishi grew deathly ill with some sort of respiratory infection no one could treat. We think it was some sort of bacterial, fungal, or parasitic infection in his apartment that infused everything in it – curtains, furniture, books, everything.

His breathing grew more labored each day, but others could enter his home and remain unaffected.

He may have been sensitized to it because he was over-exposed, remaining inside during the COVID pandemic. Or maybe it was another God thing – a push to move to Kanha full-time.

He did move to Kanha full-time and now manages the team in person *with* the team, seeing the community every day, conversing with forest officials, and more.

It was good for TTC as well as him.

What do we envision, going forward?

Remember, these are possibilities, not promises.

To enhance the full-time presence of Nishi and some of the team, we envision a permanent, physical presence (for example, a building) and more regular visits from the chairman, as well as an all-team gathering.

We plan to continue to inform, inspire, and catalyze, with our writings and grassroots projects reported in the media and published nationally and internationally. We're a small organization with big ideas and a big footprint of impact beyond our local community.

We haven't yet grown into our paws.

We look forward to fulfilling our original vision of policy impact and executive education, eco-technology use and promotion, and community programs (including K-12 education).

We plan to grow and diversify our donor base to both reduce reliance on any one donor and to raise more money with which to expand our programs. As we grow, we envision expanding our program portfolio with more profit-making opportunities in partnership with our community, e.g., through micro-entrepreneurship or product sales. The resort remains in the plans.

A new part of our vision is to become an incubation hub for EdTech and MedTech services, making them available around the world.

Whatever we do must be scalable globally, even though our current footfall is significant, with 30 villages and broad-based reach to 200,000 people (some scattered across the forest without villages). We have no doubt that what works will grow – new programs in our location, and existing programs in new locations.

Things are not perfect – they never are – but there is a light, and it is spreading.

We thank you, as always, for your support. The work we do works only one way – together.

This is not the end. It is not even the beginning of the end. But it is, perhaps, the end of the beginning. — Winston Churchill

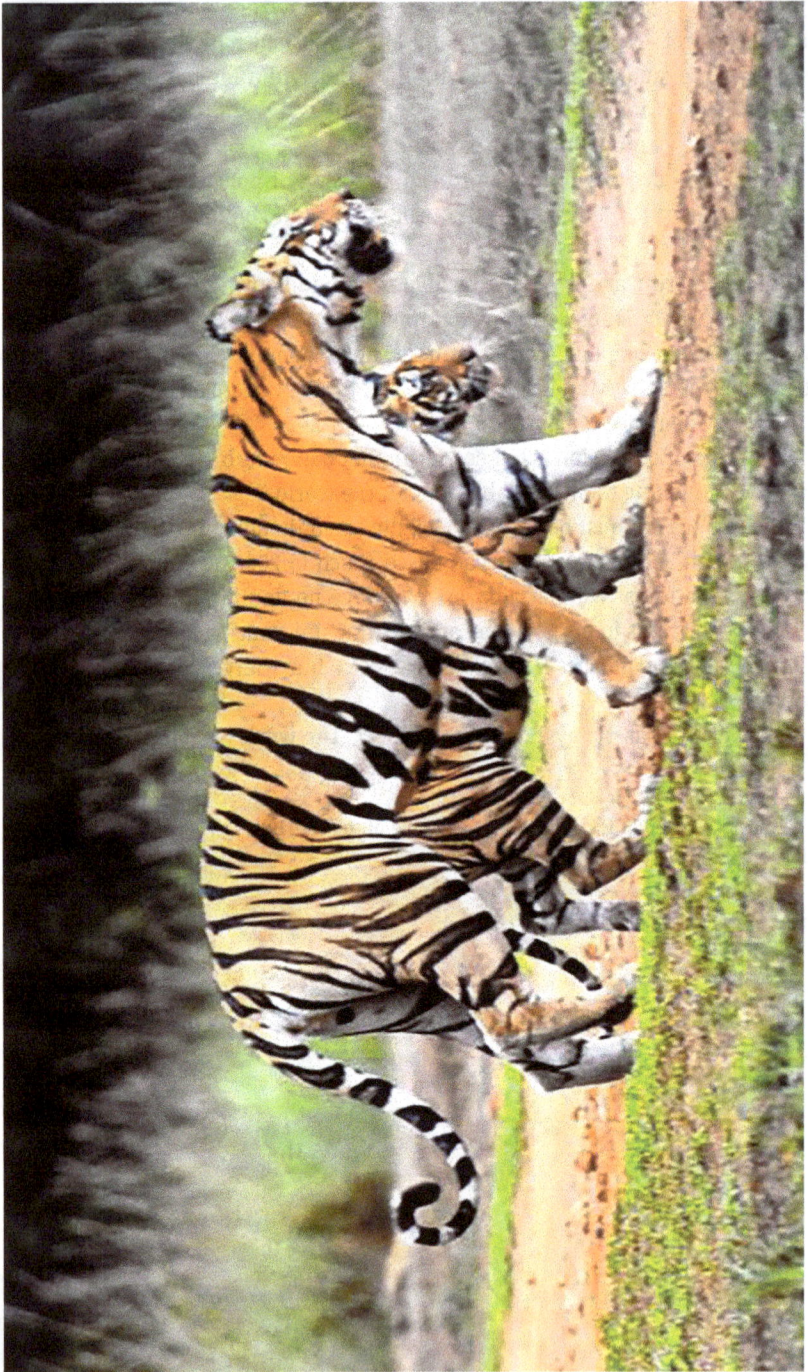

References

Anand, U. (2021, February 4). What's the Value of a Tree? Age Multiplied by INR 43.5k: SC Panel. Hindustan Times. https://www.hindustantimes.com/india-news/whats-the-value-of-a-tree-age-multiplied-by-74-5k-sc-panel-101612377235565.html.

Banerjee, P. (2015, February 1). The Roar Is Back: India's Tigers Are on The Prowl Again. The Hindustan Times. https://www.hindustantimes.com/india/the-roar-is-back-india-s-tigers-are-on-their-prowl-again/story-Q9MUCYuY8toZ9ycWfxm7lM.html.

Broz, M. (2023, February 21). Number of Photos (2023): Statistics, Facts, and Predictions. Phototutorial. https://phototutorial.com/photos-statistics/#:~:text=According%20to%20Phototutorial's%20most%20recent,and%20150.8%20billion%20per%20month.

Choudhari, A. (2023, January 2). Nagpur Set to be Branded as "Tiger Capital" for G20 Meet. Times of India Newspaper.

Dasgupta, K. (2015, February 1). How Periyar Saved Its Big Cat Population. The Hindustan Times. https://www.hindustantimes.com/india/the-roar-is-back-india-s-tigers-are-on-their-prowl-again/story-Q9MUCYuY8toZ9ycWfxm7lM.html.

Dasgupta, P. (2023). List of Tiger Reserves in India 2023, Significance, and Schemes. Adda 247 Current Affairs. https://currentaffairs.adda247.com/list-tiger-reserves-in-india-2023-significance-and-schemes/#:~:text=in%20India%202023-,Tiger%20Reserves%20in%20India%202023%3A%20The%20Guru%20Ghasidas%20National%20Park,and%20is%20located%20in%20Chhattisgarh.

Dayanidhi. (2022, August 29). Half of All Snakebite Cases in the World from India, Finds Study. Down to Earth News. https://www.downtoearth.org.in/news/health/half-of-all-snakebite-cases-in-the-world-from-india-finds-study-84581.

Economic Times. (2022, September 17). Modi Government's Contribution, Efforts to Conserve Wildlife Have Brought Positive Outcomes. https://economictimes.indiatimes.com/news/india/modi-governments-contribution-efforts-to-conserve-wildlife-have-brought-positive-outcomes/articleshow/94262789.cms.

Explore. (2014, July 31). 10 Highest Grossing National Parks. Explore Magazine. https://www.explore.com/10-highest-grossing-national-parks.

Global Snakebite Initiative (GSI). (n.d.). The Snakebite Problem. (Blog). https://www.snakebiteinitiative.org/snakebite-problem/.

Gore, A. (2013). Earth in the Balance. Abingdon, Oxfordshire, UK: Routledge.

Hawken, P., Lovins, A., Lovins, L. (2020). Natural Capitalism: Creating the Next Industrial Revolution. Washington, DC: US Green Building Council.

Hindustan Times. (2017, July 16). Saving 2 tigers gives more value than the cost of Mangalyaan! https://www.hindustantimes.com/environment/saving-2-tigers-gives-more-value-than-the-cost-of-mangalyaan/story-s17glKMyLKHeuEHzwpidZM.html.

Indian Institute of Forest Management. (2016). Economic Valuation of Kanha Tiger Reserve. (Policy brief). https://iifm.ac.in/wp-content/uploads/kanha.pdf.

Kaplan, R. & Norton, R. (1996). The Balanced Scorecard: Translating Strategy into Action. Boston, MA, USA: Harvard Business Review Press.

Khambete, A. (2019, January 9). When water kills. India Water Portal. https://admin.indiawaterportal.org/faqs/when-water-kills.

Leonard, D. & Straus, S. (1997). Putting Your Company's Whole Brain to Work. *Harvard Business Review*. 97407-PDF-ENG.

https://doi.org/10.1515/9783110783179-006

Mahaptra, D. (2020, January 10). Calculate Value of a Tree by Volume of Oxygen It Gives: SC. Times of India, p. 1.

Meadows, C. (2015). Why My Blonde Son Thought He Was Chinese: The Fusion Family. (Video8. Singapore TEDxACSIndependent. https://www.youtube.com/watch?v=e7PGMtOa-CA.

Ministry of Environment. (2016). International Conference on Recent Advances in Civil Engineering, Architecture and Environmental Engineering for Sustainable Development (CEAESD- 2016).

Mukerji, N. (2009). EDEN: Economic Development with Environmental Nurturing. (Whitepaper). Nagpur, India: The Tiger Center. https://medium.com/@Dr.CJ/eden-economic-development-with-environmental-nurturing-75713ad352d1.

Mukerji, N. (2009). Managing Natural Assets. (Whitepaper). Nagpur, India: The Tiger Center. https://medium.com/@Dr.CJ/managing-natural-assets-49e90705cdce.

Mukerji, N. (2017). EDEN-2: The Golden Triangle Model and Strategy Survey. (Whitepaper). Nagpur, India: The Tiger Center. https://medium.com/@Dr.CJ/eden-2-the-golden-triangle-model-strategy-survey-6d7b5256dbbc.

Minnesota Zoo. (ca.2004). Tiger Facts. www.mnzoo.com/education/ticadventures/ta4text/a3.htm.

Mukerji, N. (2009, updated 2017). EDEN: Economic Development with Environmental Nurturing. (Whitepaper). Nagpur, Maharashtra, India: The Tiger Center. https://medium.com/@Dr.CJ/eden-economic-development-with-environmental-nurturing-75713ad352d1.

Mukerji, N. (2017). EDEN-2: EDEN-2: The Golden Triangle Model and Strategy Survey. (Whitepaper). Nagpur, Maharashtra, India: The Tiger Center. https://medium.com/@Dr.CJ/eden-2-the-golden-triangle-model-strategy-survey-6d7b5256dbbc.

NDTV. (2022, November 25). Through USHA Silai Schools, Women Entrepreneurs Are Generating Jobs and Providing Livelihoods. https://www.ndtv.com/photos/news/through-usha-silai-schools-women-entrepreneurs-are-generating-jobs-and-providing-livelihoods-103813#goog_rewarded-and-companion-page-Adopt-a-Silai-School https://special.ndtv.com/kushalta-ke-kadam-12/adopt-a-silai-school.

New International Version Bible. (1984). Zondervan (Bible Gateway). www.biblegateway.com.

Newburger, E. (2023, January 9). The Earth's Ozone Layer is Slowly Recovering, UN Report Finds. CNBC. https://www.cnbc.com/2023/01/09/the-earths-ozone-layer-is-slowly-recovering-un-report-finds-.html#:~:text=In%20this%20NASA%20false%2Dcolor,new%20United%20Nations%20report%20says.

Pendell, R. (2022, June 14). The World's $7.8 Trillion Workplace Problem. Gallup Workplace. https://www.gallup.com/workplace/393497/world-trillion-workplace-problem.aspx.

Semler, R. (2014). How to Run a Company With (Almost) No Rules. TEDGlobal2014. https://www.ted.com/talks/ricardo_semler_how_to_run_a_company_with_almost_no_rules?language=en.

Statista. (2023). Number of Overnight, International Tourists in South Africa from 2012 to 2021. Hamburg, Germany: Statista. https://www.google.com/search?q=statista+headquarters&sxsrf=AJOqlzUvPmKDm077AA88mZ2MILGur0C8kQ%3A16769567727481&ei=N1T0Y-75HLWA3LUPttCh sAU&ved=0ahUKEwiu8a3Q7qX9AhU1ALcAHTZoCFYQ4dUDCA8&uact=5&oq=statista+headquar ters&gs_lcp=Cgxnd3Mtd2l6LXNlcnAQAzIECCMQJzIFCAAQgAQyBQgAEIYDMgUIABCGAzIF CAAQhgM6CggAEEcQ1gQQsANKBAhBGABQvQdYvQdgmAloAXABeACAATKIATKSAQExmAEAoAE ByAEIwAEB&sclient=gws-wiz-serp.

Vaidyanathan, G. (2019, October 30). India's Tigers seem to Be a Massive Success Story – Many Scientists Aren't Sure. Nature, 574, 612–616. https://www.nature.com/articles/d41586-019-03267-z.

Verma, M., Negandhi, D., Khanna, C., Edgaonkar, A., David, A., Kadelkod, G., Costanza, R., Gopal, R., Bonal, B., Yadav, S., Kumar, S. (2017). Making the Hidden Visible: Economic Valuation of Tiger

Reserves in India. Ecosystem Services, 26(A), 236–244. https://www.sciencedirect.com/science/article/abs/pii/S2212041617303339.

Verma, M., Tiwari C., Anand S., Edgaonkar, A., David, A., Kadekodi, G., Ninan K.N., Sharma P., Panda P., Thatey, Z. (2019, July). Economic Valuation of Tiger Reserves in India: Phase II. Bhopal, India: Indian Institute of Forest Management. (Research report). https://ntca.gov.in/assets/uploads/Reports/EconEval/Economic_evaluation_phaseII.pdf.

Wikipedia. Various pages accessed. https://en.wikipedia.org/wiki/Main_Page.

World Economic Forum. (2022, May). Travel and Tourism Development Index 2021: Rebuilding for a Sustainable and Resilient Future. (Insight Report). Cologny, Switzerland: World Economic Forum. https://www3.weforum.org/docs/WEF_Travel_Tourism_Development_2021.pdf.

WWF (World Wildlife Fund for Nature). (2023). Tiger Facts. https://www.worldwildlife.org/species/tiger#:~:text=The%20continental%20tigers%20currently%20include,believed%20to%20be%20functionally%20extinct.

WWF (World Wide Fund for Nature, formerly World Wildlife Fund for Nature). (2023). Up to 100 Million Sharks are Killed Annually. https://adopt.wwf.sg/species/shark#:~:text=PROTECTING%20SHARKS%20FROM%20EXTINCTION&text=But%20currently%2C%20they%20are%20under,at%20risk%20of%20extinction%20globally.

Yale School of the Environment. (2011, May 3). Sharks Worth Far More Alive Than Dead, New Study Shows. E360 Digest. https://e360.yale.edu/digest/sharks_worth_far_more_alive_than_dead_new_study_shows#:~:text=more%20than%20half%20of%20tourists,Australian%20Institute%20of%20Marine%20Sciences.

Yes Bank Strategic Government Advisory and FICCI. (2019, April). India Inbound Tourism – Unlocking the Opportunity. (Industry report). https://ficci.in/spdocument/23082/India-Inbound-Tourism-Knowledge-Paper-ficci.pdf.

List of Figures

https://doi.org/10.1515/9783110783179-007

Index

Fun Fact: Evading tigers isn't the only thing on the mind of barasingha, like the one above. During mating season, they've been known to "enhance" their antler girth with long grass. Attractive to the ladies. Hopefully not to tigers.

https://doi.org/10.1515/9783110783179-008

www.ingramcontent.com/pod-product-compliance
Lightning Source LLC
Chambersburg PA
CBHW061259220326
41599CB00028B/5711